# CONCILIUM

*Religion in the Seventies*

# CONCILIUM

## Editorial Directors

*Concilium* 118 (8/1978): Ecumenism

# AN ECUMENICAL CONFESSION OF FAITH?

Edited by

## Hans Küng and Jürgen Moltmann

A CROSSROAD BOOK

The Seabury Press · New York

1979
The Seabury Press
815 Second Avenue
New York, N.Y. 10017

Library of Congress Catalog Card Number: 79-83934
ISBN: 0-8164-0408-9
ISBN: 0-8164-2198-6 (pbk.)
Printed in the United States of America

# CONTENTS

# Part II
# What Belongs in a Future Ecumenical Creed?

# Part III
# New Ways

# Part IV
# Attempt at a Synthesis

# Editorial: Towards an Ecumenical Confession of Faith

AN ECUMENICAL confession of faith? This is a genuine question. For confession is a thoroughly anti-ecumenical concept, denoting not what unites but what divides. It is a term which describes differences and distinctions, all that separates one denomination from another; a Lutheran cannot simultaneously be a Roman Catholic or a member of the Reformed Church. The existence of different denominations is the expression—is in fact the cause of—confessional division and therefore of division between the Churches. If we want to surmount this disunity, is it not important, not of pressing necessity, to find a *common* confession of faith: *an ecumenical confession of faith?*

But at the same time, this is a difficult question. What at first sight appears simple, is, on closer examination, highly complex. For a confession of faith involves the totality of belief. But is that not perhaps an overloading of the term confession? Is it at all possible to represent the unity of faith, the community of believers, in a common creed? And if it is, in which creed? An old one perhaps? Are the confessions of faith, once used by the Church, appropriate to conditions today? Are they not historically determined, and to some extent, polemicizing statements, that could, even when they were drawn up, only imperfectly formulate the essentials of Christian belief? Isn't the ethical dimension—and in particular the whole field of social ethics—completely absent? Are the old confessions of faith an adequate response to present-day conditions in Europe and the United States, to say nothing of Africa, Asia and Latin America?

Should we not therefore try a *new* confession of faith? But is it in fact possible to formulate one in the absence of any immediate pressure to do so? Surely, however, the contemporary situation for Christianity is urgent enough to justify the attempt—particularly as a common confession of faith of the sort I have in mind has scarcely the same binding force as those of the old Church. Doesn't a new confession of faith presuppose that a considerable measure of unity has already been achieved?

This is the crux of the matter. In this *Concilium*, the reader will find a profusion of possible answers: some explore the nature and possible functions of denominational identity; some look at the different meanings attached to credal statements within the different denominational traditions; some discuss the desirability of a common confession of faith in the light of new perspectives and considerations within the different cultural traditions. Nevertheless, it is essential to establish what is essential to a new confession of faith, to what extent it accords with the *practices* and the *life* of the Churches, and how far *unity has already become a reality*. There can be no shared confession of faith without a sharing of the practical realities of daily life.

And here the church leaders—particularly those of the Catholic Church—have a grave responsibility. Considering that the foundations for unity have already been laid, do they really do enough to promote its growth? Surely they should do much more to guide their Churches towards confessional unity—a unity that can be expressed in word and activity even in the absence of a formulated confession of faith. Surely the church leaders should respond more positively to the initiatives taken at grass-roots level.

In this context the following points should be borne in mind. In many countries, at *parish level,* ecumenical practices have quite unobtrusively become established. These are the premises of confessional unity and can, in their turn, perhaps, lead to a common confession of faith. Certainly it is difficult to analyze grass-roots ecumenical practice for it can take a variety of forms and we know little of the exact details and numbers involved. Ecumenical practice can only flourish at this unofficial level but that is no reason to condemn or belittle it. Many Christians regard the division of the Churches as a scandal. Their experiences have been good ones, which have taught them that together with other Christians they believe in the same God and in Jesus Christ and that they belong to a single community of the baptized, the Spirit, belief, activity and the eucharist. This new ecumenical practice at grass-roots level gives us cause for great hope. At the same time, its dangers must not be overlooked. If the Church leadership fails to respond to the impetus towards ecumenism, it will lose control of the process and will, in the course of time be unable credibly to integrate grass-roots ecumenism into the unity of the Church.

Unofficial ecumenical activity taking place at *parish* level among committed Christians and clergy of all denominations must, therefore, be taken extremely seriously. There are numerous indications that formal unity is being anticipated by practice: inter-communion and common celebrations of the eucharist among small groups and in private houses; unconditional participation in the services and eucharists of other Churches which offer hospitality, particularly to partners in a mixed marriage; the growing number of clergy, who, although it is expressly forbidden, permit inter-denominational participation in the eucharist, hold ecumenical religious instruction and who, in theoretical and practical terms, deviate from their own Churches' official understanding of the ministry; the effectiveness and testimony of local communities, working in areas where the larger Church has little influence and where denominational differences no longer have any real meaning (university chaplaincies, groups of workers, marginal groups and socially disadvantaged communities).

If the church leaders are not prepared to legitimize such practices, then they should at least be prudent and honest enough to acknowledge their existence, to analyze their significance and to draw the necessary conclusions about their future. It would clearly be better to recognize the working of the Spirit in this growing unofficial ecumenism than to ban it altogether and thus relegate it to a no man's land between the denominations and outside the official Church.

Nor should we overlook the following considerations. Official ecumenism, whether at a *universal* or *national* level, is of only *secondary* importance. Ecumenical experience at the *local* level is not just the point of departure but the aim of *all ecumenical endeavour*. For it is only here that an ecumenical project can be transformed into ecumenical reality. The aim is not to create one huge, uniform, united Church but instead, one that is liturgically, theologically and organizationally diverse and which no longer admits the practice of excluding *any* Christian from *any* parish service.

Local ecumenical movements have the right and duty to encourage loyalty to both the Church at a local level and the Church as a whole, to further ecumenism and to allow the *greatest possible* diversity in the practical application of theological thinking. Ecumenism does not suddenly acquire legitimacy the moment it is officially sanctioned. The burden of proof rests with those who seek to prohibit or restrict it. Ecumenical activity at the local level has shown that often the real barriers to collectivity and mutual encounter between Christians are not so much doctrinal differences as an emotional attachment to particular devotional practices and a fear that their individual identity is threatened. Ecumenical activity within the local community has to try to counter these difficulties with a *new collective experience of belief,* achieved through a common celebration, prayer, activity and profession of faith.

Thus a shared and collective way of *life* can develop, and with it a shared *confession* in word and activity. That this may lead to a formulated ecumenical *credal statement* is both important and desirable. But, compared to a common life and confession, it is of but secondary importance.

HANS KÜNG
JÜRGEN MOLTMANN

# PART I

*Basic Questions*

Bernhard Lang

# Professions of Faith in the
# Old and New Testaments

PROFESSIONS of faith do not form a prominent type of text in either the Old or the New Testament. Only in two cases do we possess credal formulations in their complete liturgical context: Deuteronomy 26:1–11 and Acts 8:37. The first consists of the thanksgiving of an Israelite peasant at harvest-time, the second a neophyte's profession of faith at baptism. Without these two passages we would hardly be able to construct a proper picture of biblical professions of faith.

The other passages quoted or referred to in what follows are either allusions to credal statements or quotations from them, or are closely connected with them as far as their content is concerned. We are only able to understand passages of this kind if we try to trace them back to their original pre-literary context.

## THE OLD TESTAMENT

The Old Testament contains a whole series of credal formulations. They are classified in various groups according to whether they proclaim Yahweh's action in history, his lordship or his uniqueness. The first place has to be taken by the 'brief historical creed' of Deuteronomy 26 that has been the subject of a great deal of discussion.[1]

## The 'Historical' Confession of Faith

What has come to be regarded as the classical profession of faith runs as follows: 'A wandering Aramaean was my father; and he went down into Egypt and sojourned there, few in number; and there he became a nation, great, mighty, and populous. And the Egyptians treated us harshly, and afflicted us, and laid upon us hard bondage. Then we cried to the Lord the God of our fathers, and the Lord heard our voice, and saw our affliction, our toil, and our oppression; and the Lord brought us out of Egypt with a mighty hand and an outstretched arm, with great terror, with signs and wonders; and he brought us into this place and gave us this land, a land flowing with milk and honey' (Dt. 26:5–9). The creed is spoken by the peasant who has come to the temple at Jerusalem with a basket full of the best produce of his entire harvest, hands the basket over to a priest, and makes his profession of faith. He concludes it with the formula: 'And behold, now I bring the best [2] of the fruit of the ground, which thou, O Lord, hast given me' (v. 10). By handing over his gifts and reciting this creed the peasant has complied with an important liturgical obligation. Presumably this obligation was established by the theologians who compiled Deuteronomy during the period of the Babylonian exile in the sixth century when sacrifices could not be offered in the temple. It was in this period that it was easiest to give a new shape to the customary harvest rituals of an earlier age that were a thorn in the theologians' flesh. These earlier rituals were carried out at local sanctuaries, not at the central one, and their background was rooted in paganism and myth. The custom had been to bring the first sheaf of the grain harvest into the sanctuary, thresh it and toast the first grains. This action was interpreted as the revenge of the goddess Anat (the priest doing the threshing) on the god of death Mot (the first sheaf).[3] The Deuteronomic theologians replaced the pagan view shaped by agricultural mythology by the Israelite idea of the gift of the land by the God of the Exodus. At the same time the theologians gave expression to their idea of totality.[4] The new harvest ritual was no longer linked only to the grain harvest of April and May but to all the fruits of the earth, and thus to the grain harvest and to the olive harvest and the vintage in August and September. The idea of totality made it necessary for the text of the creed to mention in addition to 'all the fruit of the ground' (v. 2) such things as milk and honey that are not the product of tillage. Thus the peasant acknowledges that the gifts of the land go back without exception to Yahweh: they are his gift.

Deuteronomy 26 is not Israel's only 'historical' profession of faith. There is a whole series of liturgical texts that can be placed alongside the harvest creed. Prominent among them is Joshua 24. If the setting described there is more than a literary fiction we must think in terms of a regular service involving a profession of faith. This would consist of two parts. First a priest (or prophet) recounts the history of Yahweh's dealings with his people from Abraham on and asks those present to commit themselves to this God. Then comes the community's answer: 'Far be it from us that we should forsake the Lord, to serve other gods; for it is the Lord our God who brought us and our fathers up from the land of Egypt, out of the house of bondage' (vv. 16–17). There are several hymns (Ps. 44:1–8; 78; 105) that, like this passage from Joshua, recount longer or shorter extracts from the history of Yahweh's dealings with his people. At Psalm 105:5 in particular the point of this kind of summary is made clear: it reminds the people of what Yahweh has done for them and does not let them forget their sufferings in Egypt and their glorious Exodus. But the passages are so flexible that the remembrance can be extended into the time of the kings (Ps. 78) or can be confined to the take-over of the promised land (Ps. 44). This multiplicity of creeds reflects not only the variety of liturgical life but also the absence of the idea of a fixed content of faith. Because Israel had no 'teaching authority' or 'magisterium' there could be no official creed.

## The Acknowledgement of Yahweh's Lordship

Anyone who learns of Yahweh's saving deeds or experiences them in person, as did Naaman when cured of leprosy, acknowledges Yahweh's lordship with rejoicing: 'The Lord is greater than all gods' (Ex. 18:11); 'Behold, I know that there is no [mighty] God in all the earth but in Israel' (2 Kg. 5:15).[5] Formulations of this kind that do not go back to the history of Yahweh's dealings with his people are not uncommon in liturgical poetry: 'I say to the Lord, "Thou art my Lord" ' (Ps. 16:2); 'For thou, O Lord, art most high over all the earth' (Ps. 97:9); 'The Lord is king for ever and ever' (Ps. 10:16). More explicit and extended passages like Psalms 104 or 146 are not content just to affirm Yahweh's lordship. Rather they bring out what Yahweh does for mankind in general or for Israel in particular: '[The Lord] who made heaven and earth, the sea, and all that is in them; who keeps faith for ever; who executes justice for the oppressed; who gives food to the hungry. The Lord sets the prisoners free; the Lord opens the eyes of the blind. The Lord lifts up those who are bowed down; the Lord loves the righteous. The Lord watches over the sojourners, he upholds the widow and the fatherless; but the way of the wicked he brings to ruin. The Lord will reign for ever' (Ps. 146:6–10). Even outside the Psalms one encounters this kind of liturgical fragment, as in Isaiah 33:22: 'For the Lord is our judge, the Lord is our ruler, the Lord is our king; he will save us'.[6]

Among these examples of the profession of faith in the God of Israel there is one group that needs special notice: the acclamation, a brief profession of faith uttered in unison and repeated. When the prophet Elijah arranged a liturgical context with the prophets of the Canaanite god Baal fire had to fall from heaven on the sacrifice that had been prepared. To the community's surprise Elijah's prayer was heard, while Baal failed to answer the dances of his prophets. Yahweh's sacrifice suddenly caught fire: 'And when all the people saw it, they fell on their faces; and they said, "The Lord, he is God; the Lord, he is God" ' (1 Kg. 18:39). This acclamation acknowledged Yahweh, as against Baal, as the true God. Presumably the acclamation 'The Lord is God' was as common in the worship of Israel [7] as the acclamations 'The Lord is king' (or 'The Lord reigns') [8] and 'The Lord is great';[9] the latter acclamation is always accompanied by an explicit invitation to the community to join in making it.

## The Monotheistic Creed

Although Judaism is the monotheistic religion *par excellence,* a profession of faith in the one and only God was only formulated relatively late. This took place during the later period of the kings or during the Babylonian exile, in other words in the seventh or sixth century, during the Deuteronomic movement. The credal formulas run: 'The Lord is God; there is no other besides him' (Dt. 4:35); 'The Lord is God in heaven above and on the earth beneath; there is no other' (Dt. 4:39); 'The Lord is our God, the Lord is one' (Dt. 6:4). These formulas have their origin in liturgical acclamations like 'The Lord, he is God' (1 Kg. 18:39) but in Deuteronomy form part of a continuous homily. The preacher gives earlier formulas a monotheistic twist and makes them the point of his sermon. The starting point of his proclamation was a recalling of history, remembering the patriarchs chosen by Yahweh, the Exodus, and the entry into the promised land. With this history before their eyes the people, addressed collectively, were urged to recognize that there was only one God and to profess their faith in him: 'To you it was shown, that you might know that the Lord is God; there is no other besides him' (Dt. 4:35); or: 'Hear, O Israel: The Lord is our God, the Lord is one' (Dt. 6:4). This latter form with its preceding exhortation became Judaism's classical monotheistic confession of faith. It was with good reason that this and neither of the other two versions was chosen. The preceding phrase 'Hear, O Israel' acts as a reminder of the narrative context: Yahweh is not deduced from some abstract metaphysics but is the God of Israel whom his people have experienced as their rescuer and whom they acknowledge with gratitude. The original context of these monotheistic formulas seems to have been oral proclamation before they were committed to writing. Perhaps we should think in terms of sermons within the service of readings to be found in the forerunner of the Jewish synagogue. Later, monotheistic preaching was directed towards pagans too: they were brought news of the 'living God who made the heaven and the earth and the sea and all that is in them' (Acts 14:15) or they heard confessions of faith like that of Jonah: 'I am a Hebrew; and I fear the Lord, the God of heaven, who made the sea and the dry land' (Jon. 1:9).

Did the monotheistic creed have a rôle outside the context of preaching? There are several indications of this. In prayers the wish was expressed that all peoples might acknowledge: 'The Lord is God; there is no other' (1 Kg. 8:60) and 'Thou, O Lord, art God alone' (2 Kg. 19:19). And Deutero-Isaiah imagined the scene of the Egyptians as the servants of the eschatologically triumphant people of God bowing down and acknowledging: 'God is with you only, and there is no other, no god besides him' (Is. 45:14).

THE NEW TESTAMENT

The Old Testament message of the uniqueness of God, of the lordship of Yahweh and of his action in history was not very often summarized in credal formulas. With the message of the New Testament it is quite different. The profession of faith in the risen Jesus, sometimes linked with profession of faith in the one unique God,[10] is something we encounter in a bewildering profusion of concise formulas in all the writings of the New Testament.[11] Right from the start Christianity can be termed a religion centred on a creed. But at the same time there was no attempt at all to develop a uniform credal text. Rather, what strikes us is precisely the multiplicity of fresh formulations which cannot be traced back to any original exemplar. These credal texts served as hymns during worship, as acclamations or as baptismal creeds, and provided a peg for preaching by furnishing the substantial content of instruction in the faith.

## Professions of Faith in Worship

The New Testament contains an abundance of hymns such as Philippians 2:6–11 and John 1 as well as formulas that can be regarded as fragments of hymns. Two such fragments are: 'There is one God, and there is one mediator between God and men, the man Christ Jesus' (1 Tim. 2:5); 'He was manifested in the flesh, vindicated in the Spirit, seen by angels, preached among the nations, believed on in the world, taken up in glory' (1 Tim. 3:16). In one case the context indicates that what we have to do with is a baptismal creed: 'I believe that Jesus Christ is the Son of God' (Acts 8:37). This phrase is attached to the story of the conversion of the Ethiopian eunuch baptized by Philip. The original text did not contain any specific creed: the unspecified acceptance of 'the good news of Jesus' seems to have sufficed for baptism. Some of the ancient authorities for the text do however include this credal formula which is often alluded to in the New Testament.[12]

Briefer and more impressive than the baptismal creed are acclamations chanted rhythmically by the congregation. Paul (1 Cor. 12:3) quotes 'Jesus is Lord' as an acclamation and places alongside it an anti-Christian slogan, and one perhaps no less commonly used [13]: 'Jesus be cursed!' In Greek both consist of only two words and are thus very well suited to being chanted as slogans by a congregation or a crowd. In modern languages Ephesians 4:5 also sounds most easily like a slogan chanted during worship: 'One Lord, one faith, one baptism'—presumably one to be found in the service of baptism. But the cry 'Jesus is Lord' must have been heard much more often during worship, since Paul frequently alludes to it.[14] An idea of the use in the ancient world of an acclamation as a 'war cry' [15] is provided by the account of the anti-Christian demonstration in the theatre at Ephesus. The crowd was stirred up by the silversmiths, who found no customers among the Christians for their silver shrines of Artemis; and when someone wanted to speak on behalf of the Christians, 'for about two hours they all with one voice cried out, "Great is Artemis of the Ephesians!"' (Acts 19:34). Use of the acclamation has today practically died out in church, though in the form of the slogan it is well-known in advertising, politics and sport.[16] Classic examples are the Nazi Sieg Heil! and the French revolutionary slogan Guerre aux châteaux! Paix aux chaumières! ('War on the castles! Peace to the cottages!'). These examples show clearly not only the rhythmical structure of the slogan but its aggressive and hostile mood and function: slogans are chanted for Yahweh against Baal, for Artemis against Jesus, for Jesus or against him, for cottages against châteaux, for victory against the enemy.

## The Profession of Faith in Preaching and Catechesis

Although the examples of preaching to be found in Acts are literary compositions, they indicate something of the technique and subject-matter of actual preaching in the mission-field. The core of one of these sermons runs: 'The God of our fathers raised Jesus whom you killed by hanging him on a tree. God exalted him at his right hand as Leader and Saviour, to give repentance to Israel and forgiveness of sins' (Acts 5:30–31). The fact that practically the same terms are used to describe Jesus's resurrection in six other speeches in Acts [17] shows their nature as a formula and how common they were. The oldest Christian missionary sermon available to us was centred on a Christological creed and was in its substance a homily on a creed. The introduction to this Christological confession of faith varied according to the audience it was addressed to. For a Jewish audience the sermon began with Abraham and the Exodus (Acts 13:16–41), for pagans with the creation of the world (Acts 17:24), and thus from time to time with specific subjects of the pre-Christian creed. The Christological profession of faith is not something hanging in the air but supplements the content of pre-Christian belief. And of course the presupposition of the missionary preachers was that the content of the faith of Jewish Christians need not be identical with that of Christians from a pagan background. The missionary situation was opposed to the formation of a uniform, all-embracing confession of faith. The drawing up of a universally binding creed was a preoccupation not of the first missionaries but only of the theologians of a later generation.

Important first of all was the transmission of the credal core of this preaching in catechetical instruction. The fact that a fixed form of words was used in this is explicitly stated by Paul: 'Now I would remind you, brethren, *in what terms* I preached to you the gospel, which you received, in which you stand, by which you are saved, if you hold it fast—unless you believed in vain. For I delivered to you as of first importance what I also received' (1 Cor. 15:1–3a). Then he goes on to indicate what these terms were: 'that Christ died for our sins in accordance with the scriptures, that he was buried, that he was raised on the third day in accordance with the scriptures, and that he appeared to Cephas, then to the twelve' (vv. 3b–5). This text is the oldest *datable* creed in the entire New Testament and must have arisen in the period 35 to 40 A.D.

## Function and Limitations of Credal Texts

Presumably at the beginning of his letter to the Romans (Rom. 1:3–4) Paul is alluding to a credal hymn that achieved a wide circulation and was well known in Rome too: once this had been read and recognized then the reader knew from the very first lines of the letter that the writer was both Christian and orthodox. By using the creed as a kind of visiting card Paul put his Christian identity beyond doubt and won himself an introduction to and hearing among strangers. This special function of the creed is an exception. But as far as its structure is concerned it is repeated in every service and every sermon. On every occasion that a credal formula is used the Christian identity is given verbal expression and thus becomes capable of being recognized.

In the letters of the New Testament, however, credal formulations have another function. They are adopted in order to provide proof from the core of the Christian message in a context of debate or instruction. Thus in the letter to the Philippians the exhortation to humility is supported by quoting the hymn recounting how Jesus had humbled himself (Phil. 2:6–11). In the letter to the Romans the question whether believers can be condemned by God is answered in the negative by reference to a credal formulation: 'Who is to condemn? Is it Christ Jesus, who died, yes, who was raised from the dead, who is at the right hand of God, who indeed intercedes for us?' (Rom. 8:34). Thus the quotations for hymns and other credal texts do not simply serve the purposes of rhetorical embellishment but point to the irreducible basis of theology, since every argument and exhortation is derived from or legitimated by the Christological profession of faith.[18]

The confession of faith used for quotation and with its fixed form of words cannot of course guarantee Christian truth on its own. With the formula summing up the faith go the exposition and interpretation of its contents. This is particularly well demonstrated by the context of the formula quoted by Paul in 1 Corinthians 15:3–5. In arguing with those who disputed a future resurrection Paul does not just quote the credal formula against them. Rather he adopts a detailed exposition to show that the resurrection of all the dead belongs to the resurrection of Jesus that is encapsulated in the credal text. On its own the profession of faith would not have provided a corrective against the erroneous doctrine of a resurrection that was only in the present and had already happened. Rather it seems that those who preached this erroneous doctrine shared Paul's creed. In this way conflict over the true doctrine is decided not by reference to the precise words used in a creed but by its interpretation. A profession of faith the language of which is firmly established may indeed encourage the continuity and identity of belief but cannot render it secure. It is only in dispute over the correct interpretation that Christian truth can be found.

*Translated by Robert Nowell*

## Notes

1. Summaries of research: G. Wallis, 'Die geschichtliche Erfahrung und das Bekenntnis zu Jahwe im Alten Testament', *Theologische Literaturzeitung* 101 (1976), pp. 801–16; J. I. Durham, 'Credo, Ancient Israelite', in *The Interpreter's Dictionary of the Bible*, Supplementary Volume (Nashville, 1976), pp. 197–99.

2. This is how it ought to be translated, not as 'first fruits'.

3. This myth is behind Lev. 2:14, cf. G. Widengren, *Religionsphänomenologie* (Berlin, 1969), pp. 255 ff.; H. Gese, in C. M. Schröder (ed.), *Die Religionen der Menschheit*, vol. 10/1 (Stuttgart), 1970), pp. 73–74.

4. Cf. such expressions as 'all Israel' (Dt. 1:1), 'all the men of war' (Dt. 2:16), 'all his people' (2:33), 'every city' (2:34). Deuteronomy is full of expressions like these.

5. I do not take 2 Kings 5:15 as a monotheistic profession of faith.

6. There is an instructive equivalent from a source outside the Bible: 'Baal the highest is our king, our judge; none is above him', A. Caquot and others, *Textes ougaritiques* I (Paris, 1974), p. 176.

7. Cf. Ps. 100:3.

8. Ps. 93:1; 96:10; 97:1; 99:1. Cf. A. Gelston, 'A Note on YHWH MLK', *Vetus Testamentum* 16 (1966), pp. 507–12.

9. Ps. 35:27; 40:16; 70:4; Mal. 1:5.

10. Cf. 1 Cor. 8:6; Eph. 4:5–6; 1 Tim. 2:5.

11. For summaries of the present state of discussion cf. M. Rese, 'Formeln und Lieder im Neuen Testament', in *Verkündigung und Forschung* 15 (1970), pp. 75–95; H. F. Weiss, 'Bekenntnis und Uberlieferung im Neuen Testament', *Theologische Literaturzeitung* 99 (1974), pp. 321–30; H. von Campenhausen, 'Der Herrentitel Jesu und das urchristliche Bekenntnis', *Zeitschrift für die neutestamentliche Wissenschaft* 66 (1975), pp. 127–9.

Standard works: V. H. Neufeld, *The Earliest Christian Confessions* (Leiden, 1963); H. Schlier, 'Die Anfänge des christologischen Credo' in *Zur Frühgeschichte der Christologie (Quaestiones disputatae* 51) (Freiburg-im-Breisgau, 1970), pp. 13–58; H. Köster, 'Grundtypen und Kriterien frühchristlicher Glaubensbekenntnisse', in H. Köster & J. M. Robinson, *Entwicklungslinien durch die Welt des frühen Christentums* (Tübingen, 1971), pp. 191–215 (English translation, *Trajectories through early Christianity*, Philadelphia 1971); K. Wengst, *Christologische Formeln und Lieder des Urchristentums* (Gütersloh, 1972); K. Kleisch, *Das heilsgeschichtliche Credo in den Reden der Apostelgeschichte* (Cologne, 1975); H. J. van der Minde, *Schrift und Tradition bei Paulus* (Munich, 1976).

12. 1 Jn. 2:22; 4:15; 5:1, 5; Hebr. 4:14.

13. Was this slogan used to reject Jesus in conservative Jewish circles or in Christian Gnostic circles? Cf. K. Maly, '1 Kor 12:1–3, eine Regel zur Unterscheidung der Geister?' *Biblische Zeitschrift* 10 (1966), pp. 82–95; N. Brox, 'Anathema Jesus (1 Kor. 12:3)', *Biblische Zeitschrift* 12 (1968), pp. 103–11.

14. Besides 1 Cor. 12:3 there are Rom. 10:9; Phil. 2:11.

15. E. Käsemann, 'Liturgische Formeln im Neuen Testament' in *Die Reli-*

*gion in Geschichte und Gegenwart,* vol II (Tübingen,³1958), cols 993–96 (col 994 quoted here).

16. H. Schultz, 'Verse in Politik und Werbung', *Neue Rundschau* (1972), pp. 514–27.

17. Acts 2:24, 3:15; 4:10; 10:40; 13:30; 17:31.

18. G. Lohfink, 'Erzählung als Theologie', *Stimmen der Zeit* 192 (1974), pp. 521–32: the reference here is to pp. 524–25.

Jürgen Moltmann

# The Confession of Jesus Christ:
# A Biblical Theological Consideration

## I

CHRISTIAN faith has from the very beginning been a confessing faith. The confession of Jesus Christ forms a constitutive part of this faith. Without this confession, it ceases to be Christian faith. The public confession of Jesus Christ is the divine definition of this faith. That is why a denial of Jesus Christ is the sign of an absence of faith. Confession or denial point to the being or non-being of faith.

Christ has also from the very beginning been confessed with constantly new words, images and gestures. He has been confessed in many different ways and forms, some of them mutually contradictory, in the different periods of history, in the many and varied civilizations on earth and on the hostile fronts of social and political conflicts. Where is the common ground between all these different confessions? What safeguards the community of those confessing the same faith? At every period of history, these questions confront Christians: Who is Christ for us in truth? Who are we for him? What challenges us? How can we confess him?

It is possible to safeguard the community in the confession of faith by preserving the unchangeable nature of the formulae so that it can at once be known what is confessed by all Christians everywhere and at all times. The Apostles' Creed has, for example, been repeated again and again in Christian services for centuries and has acted as a safeguard for the continuity of the confession of faith in time and the community of believers in space. But do modern industrial workers mean the same as mediaeval kings when they say this creed? Apart from the sound of the words, what connection is there between the starving slum-dweller in a basic community in Sao Paulo and the rich Christian in a European city church? The shared ritual points to a community of faith, but it does not necessarily bring it about.

With all due respect for the Sunday confession of faith together with all Christians on earth, we are bound to question what this means today. It is precisely for this reason that Christians have everywhere and at all times developed new confessions of faith. The Apostles' Creed, for example, has often been 'modernized', not necessarily to fit in with fashion, but rather to give a contemporary character to the confession of faith as a response to the challenges of the period. The contemporary character of the confession of faith is as important as its continuity, because otherwise the decision of faith is no longer obligatory.

It would seem that it is only possible to have one at the expense of the other. Continuity is found in unchanging formulae and a contemporary character is only found in changing formulae. Community in the confession of faith with all Christians everywhere and at all times can only be achieved at the price of abstraction. An actual community of all believers united in the decisive questions in a contemporary situation can only be achieved at the price of partiality.

This gives rise to a real dilemma that cannot simply be suppressed. The average universality of Church statements helps no one. They frequently aim to do justice to everyone and end by doing justice to no one. Christian faith must be confessed communally and in common with all Christians everywhere and at all times. It must also be confessed here and now in an unrepeatable way concretely and with individual decision. The uniquely contemporary confession *in statu confessionis* cannot be universal. This universal confession *in communione ecclesiae* cannot be contemporary.

It is certainly possible to combine the universal and the contemporary in a suitable way in those statements that are halfway between the common confession and the contemporary confession, but the dilemma can only be overcome if the subject changes in the confession of Jesus Christ, in other words, if it is not simply believers who are confessing universally and contemporarily Christ in community and as individuals, but if it is first and foremost Christ himself who is confessing his own to his heavenly Father.

This confession of Jesus Christ means in the first place his confession to us and only then, in the second place, our confession to him. He is our witness before we can become his witnesses. Without his confession before God, our confession in the presence of our fellow-men will continue to be empty and vague. Christ is our divine confessor: 'Everyone who confesses me before men, I will confess before my Father who is in heaven, but whoever denies me before men, I will also deny before my Father who is in heaven' (Mt. 10:32, 33; Lk. 12:8; cf. Rev. 3:5).

Our confession of Christ must therefore be orientated towards the confessing Christ. The strength and the community of our confessing faith is to be found in his confession to us. In the different periods of history, in the many and varied civilizations on earth and on the hostile fronts of social and political conflicts, only he forms the common link. This is clear from the fact that, in the history of Christian faith and its confession, only the name of Jesus has stood firm. The titles expressing his dignity, effects, person and significance—all these are variable. Titles such as Son of Joseph or Son of David have disappeared and new titles have emerged—Logos, Representative, Liberator and so on. The name of Jesus is not translatable, whereas the titles of Jesus can be translated into any language. With regard to Jesus, confessions of faith are unchangeable. With regard to the titles of Christ, they are open and changeable. Nonetheless, the old titles and the new ones must be related to the person and his unique history—the person who is called by the name of Jesus—and they must be understood in the light of that person. The Christ, the Lord, the Liberator is Jesus. What hope, lordship and liberation is in truth is therefore revealed through him, his life and his death, not through our dreams. The subject determines the predicates that we give him on the basis of our experience of faith and our hope. With our predicates and titles we anticipate the kingdom in which Jesus is the truth and the life for all men and in which 'every tongue will confess that Jesus Christ is Lord, to the glory of God the Father' (Phil. 2:11). Through their structure, their fixed point in the name of Jesus and their openness to new titles of Christ and predicates of the future, our confessions of faith reveal the eschatological tension between the cross and the kingdom in which we now exist and believe.

II

Witness, confession and denial—these are terms used in litigation. Witness is not borne to feelings and cordial expressions are not confessed. If witness is borne to the great acts of God and God's lordship over the world is confessed in the stories of the Old Testament, this means that the history of Israel was seen to take place in the great court of justice of the world. The God of Israel was believed by the Old

Testament authors to have been engaged in a lawsuit with the gods of other peoples for his property, the earth, which he created, and man, who was his image. The Second Isaiah developed this understanding of history as a lawsuit between God and the gods in his court speeches (Is. 43:9–13; 44:7–11). The peoples bear witness to their gods, but 'You are my witnesses, says the Lord' (Is. 43:10, 12; 44:8). Yahweh asks: 'Is there a God besides me?' (Is. 44: 8). Israel should bear witness to their God by telling the peoples about his faithfulness and proclaiming what is to come and the fulfilment of their God's promises. Israel's call to bear witness to the peoples in their God's fight against the gods for lordship over the world was in principle unlimited: 'I will give you as a light to the nations, that my salvation may reach to the end of the earth' (Is. 49:6; cf. 42:6). The confession of the one true God (true because of his faithfulness) by Israel bearing witness is present in God's fight in the history of the world against the gods. This fight for lordship over the world is conducted by God's people bearing witness in their lives to their God's faithfulness and his promise. They have experienced his faithfulness and they believe in his promise and can therefore bear witness to them. Through this witness borne by the people of Israel, other people were set free from gods and demons and led to the truth of the one God.

It is against this Old Testament background that Jesus is called the 'faithful witness' or the 'true witness' (Rev. 1:5; 3:14). He was sent into the world 'to bear witness to the truth' (Jn. 18:37) and was for this reason called the true witness in the New Testament. In this vocation, he proved to be reliable, because he fulfilled it in his suffering and death. It was for this reason that he was called the faithful witness. Finally, Jesus was the divine witness to the truth that sets men free from godless laws and powers. By bearing witness to this liberating truth of God, Jesus in fact sets captives free.

In the Second Isaiah there is a difference between God and the people, between the one to whom witness is borne and the witnesses. In the New Testament, however, the witness and that to which he bears witness are so closely united that Jesus bears witness to the Father by revealing himself as the Son (Jn. 8:12 ff). It is for this reason that he is called the one witness in the Gospel of John. He comes from the truth to which he bears witness, so that his witness is the truth itself. His witness for God's truth is his witness to himself and his self-witness is the witness of the one who sent him. The Holy Spirit also bears witness to him, as do those who confess him in the Spirit (Jn. 15:26).

There was another difference present in Deutero-Isaiah—the difference between the witness borne before the court and the judgment of the court—ceases to exist and the witness borne for God's truth before the court of justice of the world becomes the court of justice of the world on the basis of the divine truth of the witness borne. The witness borne and the court of law thus coincide. The divine witness becomes the judge and the judges become the accused and the acquitted. The messianic time which, according to Isaiah, begins with the lawsuit between God and the gods, becomes the last hour. According to John, the last judgment has already taken place in the witness borne by Jesus Christ—whoever believes is not condemned, but whoever does not believe is already condemned. This is a vast trinitarian view of the witness borne and the confession made by the Father, the Son and the Holy Spirit. The world and all men are involved in this trinitarian process of bearing witness by God himself.

The synoptic gospels and Paul's letters provide us with other ideas of bearing witness and confession of faith. These ideas are, as it were, halfway between the difference between God and the people of his witnesses in Isaiah and the identity between the Father to whom witness is borne and the Son who bears witness in John. In the synoptics and Paul, the object of the witness borne by Jesus is the kingdom of God. As the Messiah, Jesus bears witness to the kingdom of God and, by preaching the gospel to the poor, eating with sinners and healing the sick, also brings it about. He calls disciples, who share in his messianic mission and proclaim the gospel of the kingdom to the whole world 'as a testimony to all nations' (Mt. 24:14). Jesus also completes his messianic witness by his good confession before Pilate and the witness that he bears by his death (Mk. 14:63; Mt. 26:65). His disciples are accused and tortured, similarly to bear witness to the people (Mt. 10: 18). Like Jesus' own witness, that of the disciples also has the power to set believers free and the opposite effect on non-believers, who are to be condemned at the last judgment. This is a messianic view of the historical process of bearing witness to the future of God. The gospel is a mediating witness. In the gospel, God's kingdom and judgment are present in history. Man's salvation and disaster are therefore decided in the gospel. Christian faith, we may conclude from this brief survey, is a faith that confesses and bears witness. The confession of the gospel constitutes its eschatological structure.

III

Whichever line is followed in the New Testament—the identification in the fourth gospel of the divine witness with the God to whom witness is borne or the mediation of both by the gospel in the synoptic and Pauline traditions—the witness borne by the witnesses of Christ always gains ground by the witness of Christ himself.

Christ's witness is a public witness of liberating truth. The witness of this truth therefore also takes place in public, in order to set men free from public lies and public fear. The faith of Nicodemus, who believed secretly, privately and 'by night', is not Christian faith. Calvin pointed this out clearly enough to the humanist sympathizers of the Reformation. An obstacle to the public and witness-bearing character and therefore to the very substance of Christian faith is raised by modern political science, with its emphasis on religion as a purely private affair. Christian faith is therefore bound to insist on its right to be a public religion. If it is denied that right, it suffers. Then it can only bear public witness to the truth that sets men free by suffering and resistance.

The witness borne by Christ is an undivided witness of healing truth. In the same way, the witness borne by Christians is also undivided. It can, moreover, leave out no aspect of life. The restriction of this Christian witness to a purely religious, a private or an interior sphere is a reduction that has a harmful effect on the witness of salvation. If the witness is divided, Christ is divided. This is a 'pious' denial of the whole Christ. Christ is the 'true witness' because he bore witness to the truth. He is the 'faithful witness' because he bore witness to the truth to the point of death. In the same way, the witness borne by Christians is not only a witness in words, but also a witness of their entire lives and faithfulness to the point of death. There can be no living witness without life and death bearing witness. Confessing and imitating Christ are inseparable: this was the message of the Conference of the World Council of Churches at Nairobi, 1975 (Section I). They are two sides of the coin of the same Christian life. It is only in imitating Christ that one can really know him personally. It is only in confessing him that one can imitate him and deny oneself.

Where, then, is Christ confessed today? The theological answer to this question is: Christ is confessed in the Holy Spirit and by him. This is an extremely practical answer, because the Holy Spirit is the power in history of the new creation. He is the spirit of liberation from slavery and the power of resurrection from sin and death.

Christ is therefore confessed where the power of the new creation is active. He is confessed where prisoners liberate themselves from oppression. He is confessed where men no longer give themselves over to death, but hope for the victory of life. This is not a purely polemical answer, since where the power of the new creation is active, the resistance offered by the power of the old world stiffens. Where the oppressed try to set themselves free, the power of the oppressors becomes harder. Where men rise again to life, the shadow of death grows in size. This clearly means that Christ is confessed today and witness is borne to him in the struggle of the power of the kingdom of God against the godless power of death. Isaiah had this in mind when he called on the people of God to bear witness in the legal battle between God and the gods. Witnesses are only used in battle. In the struggle between truth and lie, freedom and oppression, life and death, these witnesses should stand up for truth, freedom and life. The 'gods', against whom Isaiah's witnesses testified and whose nothingness has to be revealed today if Christ is to be confessed as truth, freedom and life, are not only the religious idols and demons, but the deified powers of race, sex, the state and capital. It is the demon of power itself that terrorizes men and to which millions are sacrificed. Where the Spirit of the Lord is, however, witness is borne to freedom from fear and aggression.

How is Christ confessed today? It is clear from the history of Israel and the apostles that Christ has always been confessed in word and deed, in deed and suffering, in suffering and silence and in silence and dying. The unity of word and deed is self-evident when the whole of life is called to witness. The unity of deed and suffering results from this. The suffering and silence of those who bear witness to Christ is a surprising experience throughout the entire history of the Christian martyrs. The blood of the martyrs is the seed of the Church.

It is therefore essential to trust in the Holy Spirit as the divine witness to the truth of Christ, because it is God who uses the word and the deed, the deed and the suffering, the suffering and the silence and the silence and the dying as a witness to convince others. Christians are not alone with their bearing of witness in a hostile world. They are situated, with all their possibilities and also their difficulties, within the history of God who is three in one and who bears witness to himself. The Holy Spirit is their witness in their speaking and silence, acting and suffering. That is why witness can be borne without fear and very frankly: 'Do not be anxious how you are to speak or what you are to say, for what you are to say will be given to you in that hour' (Mt. 10: 19); 'the Holy Spirit will teach you in that very hour what you ought to say' (Lk. 12:12). The confession of Christians to Jesus Christ is borne up by his confession to them and it is fundamentally only a little human response. The confession of Jesus Christ to them is accepted by the witness borne by the Holy Spirit, who brings about the new creation.

*Translated by David Smith*

Alasdair Heron

# The Historically Conditioned
# Character of the Apostles' Creed

FEW ideas have worked so powerfully in modern theology as that of 'history', and perhaps none has been used in such a variety of ways, or with such apparently contradictory consequences. On the one hand, it is now a commonplace that the Bible itself and all subsequent doctrinal formulations are 'historically conditioned'; that they must be understood in their historical context rather than simply as timeless expressions of eternal truth; and that therefore they need to be reinterpreted and restated if their meaning is to be grasped and appropriated in our modern world. On the other hand, much recent theology has stressed that history itself is a matter of central theological significance; that Old and New Testament alike witness to the activity of God in history; that the gospel is grounded and centred in the history of Jesus; and that the movement of history as a whole is part of that same story.

In principle there need be no conflict between these two emphases on history: they are, or at least can be, mutually supportive. The first guards against that eternalizing or absolutizing of the historical which would deny or distort its contingent character. The second stands against the opposite temptation to evacuate history itself of its meaning and to reduce it to the transient play of insubstantial shadows. Together they reflect the dialectic at the heart of the gospel, proclaiming as it does the presence of God as man in the world in the person of Christ.

Problems do, however, arise if either of these approaches is followed to the exclusion of the other. When one comes, as in this paper, to speak of something as 'historically conditioned', it is as well to take note of the pitfalls which may lie ahead. The first and most dangerous of these—and one which has claimed many victims—is a premature equation of *conditionedness* with *limitedness*. As an historical product the Apostles' Creed is open to investigation in the light of the circumstances in which it came into being, the purposes it was intended to serve, and the uses to which it then came to be put. This is all part of its conditionedness; but how far it is limited by that background is a distinct question, which cannot be settled *a priori* and must rather be the subject of further investigation. In particular it is necessary to avoid any hasty dismissal of it as *merely* 'an historical formulation' in at least three respects. 1. This creed, like any other product of history, cannot validly be dissolved away without remainder into the background out of which it came, as if it had no identity or importance of its own. What may be called 'aetiological reductionism' is as fallacious here as elsewhere: it issues, not in *explanation*, but in *explaining away*. 2. The fact that the creed emerged at a particular time and in a particular situation certainly *raises* but cannot *decide* the question whether it may have value and relevance for other times and different situations. Continuity, even through degrees of transformation, is as much a part of history as discontinuity and contrast, and cannot properly be left out of account. 3. The creed does not belong to the origins of the Church, but to the post-canonical era. By itself, however, this does not justify its relegation to the category of theological *adiaphora*. No doubt Roman Catholics are less likely to treat it in this fashion than are those Protestants whose religion, unlike that of Luther and Calvin, rests on the narrowest possible interpretation of *sola Scriptura;* nonetheless, the point deserves to be made! A proper subordination of creeds and confessions of all kinds to the witness of Scripture does circumscribe and delimit their authority; but that is not to destroy that authority altogether, but rather to establish it on its authentic foundation.

With these qualifications in mind, I should like in the rest of this paper *first* to sketch the history of the development of the Apostles' Creed, and *second* to indicate some questions which that history raises for the Church today.[1]

It must be said at once that the name 'Apostles' Creed' is misleading. By the fourth century at the latest there was a legend that the Apostles had composed a creed, and it is to that legend that we owe this title. Again, it is still sometimes assumed that this creed belongs in its totality to the age of the ancient, undivided Church, and that on this basis it stands alongside the Nicene Creed.[2] The true position is rather different.

It seems from the available evidence that the Apostles' Creed in its present form was only finally drawn up in Gaul in the seventh or eighth century. It was in fact a provincial Western confession, developed, like other such formulae, for catechetical and liturgical use. By stages which today can no longer be clearly traced, but which doubtless reflect the influence of Gallican liturgy on the Italian Church in the centuries after Charlemagne, it eventually came to be accepted in Rome and throughout the Western Church, taking its place alongside the Nicene Creed. This place it retained even in the main Churches of the Reformation; for Lutheran, Reformed and Anglican alike continued to use it, though commonly stressing that it was *ancient* rather than *apostolic*. It was, however, eclipsed to some degree by the attention given by these Churches in the sixteenth and seventeenth centuries to the drafting of fresh confessional standards. Today among the various Protestant and Anglican traditions there are those which ascribe to this creed a distinctive authority; others which acknowledge and use it liturgically, but which define their confessional position by reference to other documents; and others again which would be hard put to it to say what status, if any, they believe it to have. So it can correctly be said of the creed as it stands that it was never universally accepted throughout the entire Church, and that there is today a fair variety of opinion about its standing.

This history of the creed does not, however, begin with its final formulation. Behind it lay a process of development which casts a rather different light upon it, and indicates that in substance it is much more ancient than we have just suggested. The greater part of it can already be traced in the questions put to those being baptized in Rome early in the third century as reported by Hippolytus, *Apostolic Tradition* xxi:

Do you believe in God the Father Almighty?
Do you believe in Christ Jesus the Son of God,
Who was born by the Holy Spirit from the Virgin Mary,
Who was crucified under Pontius Pilate and died and rose again on the third day living from the dead, and ascended into the heavens and sat down on the right hand of the Father,
and will come to judge the living and the dead?
Do you believe in the Holy Spirit, the holy Church,
and the resurrection of the flesh?

Much the same pattern, but now cast in declaratory rather than interrogative form, is to be found in the Old Roman Creed (R), attested towards the end of the fourth century by Rufinus in his *Commentarius in Symbolum Apostolorum*, and probably also by Marcellus of Ancyra in his *Apologia* at the Roman synod of 340 (Epiphanius, *Panarion* 72.3). It is not impossible that R itself dates from the third century. As reconstructed by Kelly (*op.cit.*, p. 102) from Rufinus, it runs:

I believe in God the Father Almighty;
and in Christ Jesus, His only Son, our Lord,
Who was born from the Holy Spirit and the Virgin Mary,
Who under Pontius Pilate was crucified and buried, on the third day
rose again from the dead, ascended to heaven,
sits at the right hand of the Father,
whence He will come to judge the living and the dead;
and in the Holy Spirit,
the holy Church,
the remission of sins,
the resurrection of the flesh.

Marcellus' text is in Greek rather than Latin, and includes, after 'the resurrection of the flesh', the final clause, 'life eternal'; oterhwise it displays only minor verbal differences from Rufinus'.

R is only one of a number of similar but not entirely identical creeds which can be traced in Italy, North Africa, Spain and Gaul from the fourth century onwards, and there can be no serious doubt that it is either the direct ancestor of T (the Apostles' Creed) or an earlier member of the same family. The points in which T differs from it are either minor or explicable as offering clarifications made desirable by the needs of controversy or the demands of piety. The most significant of these additions or changes in T are: 'Creator of heaven and earth', 'conceived by the Holy Spirit, born of the Virgin Mary', Christ's descent into hell, 'catholic' applied to the Church, 'the communion of the saints' and 'eternal life'. These are in fact the clues which, when taken together, indicate that T was finally formulated in seventh- or eighth-century Gaul; for while these and similar phrases are attested in much older documents, it is in Gaul at that date that the clearest parallel combinations of them can be found.

These various creeds represent the forms in which the main points of the faith were taught and affirmed. It need not surprise us that these forms varied to some extent from one place or time to another. Different local churches would assess each other's belief, if the need to do so arose, not by whether their creeds were verbally identical, but by whether they recognizably expressed the same faith. The development of conciliar theology from Nicaea onwards, however, brought understandable pressure for credal uniformity; and this eventually led in the West as in the East to the general acceptance of the Nicene Creed (C), especially in the eucharistic liturgy (though in Rome itself this did not come about until 1014). The same kind of desire for uniformity led in the Carolingian Empire to the acceptance of the Gallican T in Rome and throughout the West, so that it eventually displaced the other local descendants of R. This descendant of R thus entered at last into the heritage of R itself—a heritage which can be traced back to the third century. So while the apostolic status once ascribed to it must now be admitted to be unwarranted, T nevertheless stands as the one representative of the ancient Western credal formulations which is still in current use. It can claim a far greater antiquity than its own relatively late date might at first seem to suggest; and while in ancestry and formulation it is a distinctively Western product, the faith it affirms was indisputably as much that of the East as of the West.[3] To this extent, its potential ecumenical significance is perhaps rather greater than its historical origins indicate, in spite of the reservations with which the East has traditionally regarded it. In addition, its more kerygmatic tone as compared with the more dogmatic style of the Nicene Creed makes it at the very least a valuable complement to C, and may even give it certain advantages.

There are however other questions which arise not so much from the 'late' or 'western' character of the creed, but out of the contrast between its antiquity and the needs of today. Space permits only the briefest indication of some of these issues as a contribution to discussion.

1. In the ancient Church, credal formulae served both a liturgical and a catechetical purpose.[4] Today it is hard to suppress the feeling that these two aims have become more and more separated, so that it may often seem easier to affirm such a creed as this in *worship* than to use it in *teaching*. It may be further suggested that the end result of any such tendency can only be to evacuate it of liturgical meaning as well; and it would seem that this stage has already been reached in those Protestant Churches which in effect no longer use it.

2. All the early creeds, including this one, reflected the particular emphases which were then perceived to be central and fundamental to the Christian faith. In the intervening centuries other theological issues have somewhat altered the landscape—the identity and location of the Church itself, the status of the Bible, the shape of Christian life in the world, to name but three obvious examples. New challenges evoke new responses, illustrated by such varied instances as the Reformation

*Confessions,* the Tridentine *Profession of Faith,* the *Declaration of Barmen* and the recent *Common Catechism.* Moreover, the accessibility and relevance not only of individual points in this creed,[5] but of this kind of formula as such to modern laypeople can be disputed. There is at the least a certain communication-gap to be bridged.

3. In the ancient Church, local creeds such as R, though varying from place to place, gave expression to what was recognisable as the common faith of the Church catholic. Today the use of the same creed, even this one, by different Churches appears to be compatible with the conviction on both sides that there are differences in belief sufficient to keep them out of communion with each other. The ancient inheritance which it preserves does not in itself seem to be enough to enable, let alone guarantee, mutual recognition—either because it does not include all that is felt to be necessary, or because what it does say can be interpreted in very different ways.

These and similar problems must, I believe, be taken seriously. Starting from them, however, it is possible to move in either of two quite different directions. One may conclude that the age of 'credal Christianity', or at least of the Apostles' Creed, is passing or past; that the creed itself is now an ancient monument, to be venerated, no doubt, and visited on holidays, but no longer suitable for everyday use; and that we must seek for common Christian affirmations and bases for ecumenical understanding elsewhere. On this view, the historical conditionedness of the creed is at the same time an historical limitation which renders it inaccessible for all practical purposes. Alternatively, one may hold that a rediscovery in our own day of the full range and depth of the faith it articulates is the key alike to the necessary reintegration of worship and belief, and to the overcoming of our confessional divisions. In that case, the Apostles' Creed may be expected to have a future as well as a past, and the weight placed upon it in some modern ecumenical dialogue will be justified, at least in hope.

The choice between these views does not have to do primarily with the authority or status of this creed in itself. The question is rather about the standing of the faith of the early Church as a support and guide for our faith today. To that question many different answers have been given, either explicitly or implicitly. They range, with a great variety of nuances, from a virtual canonization of the early Church to a more or less unqualified rejection of its relevance and authority alike. Between these two extremes there lies an area in which perhaps some broad (though certainly not universal) ecumenical agreement might be found on some such basis as this. Despite the passing of time, the new and major questions which have since arisen, and the changes in our horizons and modes of communication, the Christian faith today is not a different one from that of the early Church. The major issues which it was compelled to clarify are still with us, and its classical formulations set up signposts which we ignore at our peril. We must certainly do more than merely repeat them; but we dare not do less in either our worship or our teaching.

On this basis, the Apostles' Creed will neither be treated as the final, exhaustive and definitive summary of the faith nor dismissed as a purely *passé* expression of it. Rather it will be seen as 'historical' in the double sense of having been forged under particular circumstances at a particular stage in the Church's history, and of having a continuing role to play in that history today and in the future. To some, this will seem to claim too little for it; to others, it will appear to claim too much. But perhaps 'claim' is in any case the wrong word: it is not a matter of what is to be claimed by or on behalf of the creed, but of what it has to offer the Churches today. In spite of all historical qualifications, it offers a lasting witness to the faith once delivered, an enduring point of reference and orientation handed down to us by those who went before.

### Notes

1. The history of the Apostles' Creed is surveyed in detail by J. N. D. Kelly, *Early Christian Creeds* (London, [2]1960); also P. Smulders, 'Some Riddles in the Apostles' Creed', *Bijdragen* 31 (1970), pp. 234–60.

2. The Nicene Creed used today is not the creed of Nicaea (325) but a different and fuller formula which was presented at Chalcedon (451) as having been approved by the Council of Constantinople (381). For convenience it is commonly called C; the Apostles' Creed, T; and the Old Roman Creed which we mention below, R. On the origins of C cf. Kelly, op. cit., pp. 296–331.

3. The two points at which T adds significantly to what is in C are the descent into hell and the communion of the saints; cf. Kelly, op. cit., pp. 378–83, 388–97. Neither theme is peculiarly Western, though *credal* affirmation of the latter appears to be characteristically Gallican.

4. This general point still stands even if Smulders is right in arguing (op. cit., pp. 238–39) that catechetical instruction in the West (unlike the East) was not based closely on creeds.

5. For example, it is still uncertain what *sanctorum communio* originally meant—communion *with the saints* or *in the holy things?* In addition there is the further question of how far we today are bound by the original sense (if it can be established) or free to choose other possible meanings which the words themselves are capable of bearing. We cannot here explore the complex hermeneutical problems which this question raises; but it deserves to be mentioned.

Charles Kannengiesser

# Nicaea 325 in the History
# of Christendom

## THE POLITICAL DECISION

*The Will of the Emperor*

THIS first 'ecumenical' council would never have taken place without Constantine's wish and deliberate decision. Not that the Churches had waited for the 'liberator' from Gallic parts to set up a synodal practice. In the East particularly, this had been a major factor in assuring their prosperity both in calm times and in the troubled years of the third century. In the West, Constantine himself had felt the strength of this ecclesiastical institution after his victory over Maxentius. In order to secure the support of the Christians, who were then both numerous and remarkably well-organized, he had been lavish in bestowal of gifts on the bishops of Rome and Carthage. Once involved in the Donatist quarrel, which seriously divided the episcopate of North Africa and threatened religious peace even in Gaul, he had not hesitated to implement the decisions of the Synod of Arles in 314 by brutal recourse to armed force in order to apply the anti-Donatist decrees promulgated by the synod.

After his victory over Licinius on 18 September 324, which left him sole ruler and supreme pontiff of the Roman world, he had no need of special inspiration from the Holy Spirit, let alone of any encouragement from the pope of Rome, who had stood aside from the quarrel, to order the necessary dispositions to ensure peace in religious matters throughout the length and breadth of his empire. In fact, the 'ecumenicity' of Nicaea stems not from the greater number of council fathers involved, compared with earlier synods in both East and West,[1] nor from the normative value of its 'faith' and its decrees, applied with increasing vigour till the late fourth century, and at the more important imperial councils of the following century;[2] both the greater numbers taking part and the universally accepted 'normativity' of Nicaea rather indicate, on the twin levels of society and law, the importance of this historical encounter between the synodal practice of the Christian episcopate and Constantine's political strategy. For the imperial warrior, the inheritor of the administration of Diocletian, with its four Prefects of the Praetorium (for the East, Illyria, Italy-North Africa and Gaul-Spain-Britain), its twelve Vicars governing the twelve (civil!) Dioceses that made up the Prefectures, and its 101 Provinces grouped in these Dioceses, the sacred 'concord' specially favourable at the outset of a reign, could not but be both 'ecumenical' and assured by the emperor in person.

## Combined Interests

In our laicized world of the last quarter of the twentieth century, with the Churches scattered and progressively shrivelled by secularist pressure, be it totalitarian or liberal, we need to make a special effort to understand the combination of religious and political interests that came together at Nicaea. Constantine had no real need to justify himself to the bishops for interfering in their affairs. After the dark period of persecuting princes, he inaugurated the era of imperial protectors of the Church. The bishops could only gain from sharing his ideal of peace and unity, which had been inspired by the official religion of the Empire since its inception. 325 saw the christianization of a form of monarchy unanimously celebrated in messianic terms by pagans and Christians alike when it was embodied in Augustus, its distant founder: it was no accident that, at the opening session of the synod of Nicaea, there was a solemn reading from the famous prophecy of Cumes recorded by Virgil in the fourth eclogue of the *Bucolics*.[3] Homage was paid to the supreme God of the Empire, henceforth the God of the Christians, to bring down his blessing on the whole *Oikouménè*, the 'land inhabited' by the fifty million subjects of the Roman Empire. Reading the letters dictated by Constantine on the occasion of this assembly of bishops, which decisively took charge of the eastern Empire, and contemporary writings of the chief dignitaries of the Church, the difference in their styles is striking, but equally so is the similarity of their political and religious aspirations. The 'ecumenical' spirit proclaimed by the bishops for the sake of spiritual and religious hegemony of the Churches in the universal unity of the Empire finds an exact correspondence in the no less 'ecumenical'—though in a different sense—views of Constantine. Something similar had happened on a smaller scale some fifty years earlier, in 272–73, when the Emperor Aurelian, pausing at Antioch after his victory over Queen Zenobia and the kingdom of Palmyra, had to decide the issue of the conflict between the majority of the faithful of the Church of Antioch and the still numerous followers of Paul of Samosatos, former bishop and adviser to Queen Zenobia, who had been deposed by a celebrated synod in 268, the year Aurelian's predecessor Gallian died. The members of this synod had addressed their synodal letter, announcing the deposing of Paul, to '. . . all those who exercise with us the ministry over the inhabited earth (*oikoumènè*)'. Aurelian himself decided that the orthodox party, which had the right to the episcopal throne, was simply the one that recognized the bishop of *Rome*. Here two outlooks clashed: that of the third-century bishops, strongly rooted in the traditions proper to each local metropolis, but witnessing to the universal Church of the end of time, and therefore committed to an eschatological ecumenism, which imposed a duty of ensuring peace among the different groups of 'successors of the Apostles' in the *Oikoumènè* through exchange of numerous letters and the holding of regional synods; and that of the civil and military centralism of Roman administration, which introduced the synodal regime of the Christian East to a view of unity it had not previously seen in this way.[4] At Nicaea, these two outlooks were to combine into one whole.

## A State Religion

Working through Christianity, Constantine succeeded in giving the reunified Empire a new sort of internal cohesion. After his death in 337, there was a return to separate rulers for the Eastern and Western parts of the Empire. Then Theodosius I succeeded, for the last time, in making himself sole master of the *Oikoumènè*, from 379 to 395. In a direct line from the logic of Nicaea, and in the face of the traditional tolerance of the old religion of Rome, he proclaimed Christianity the sole official religion of the Empire. After this, the only occasions on which the ideal of a unanimous unity, extended to the boundaries of the 'inhabited lands', was put into practice were the 'ecumenical' synods organized at Ephesus in 431 and Chalcedon twenty years later.

For its part, the Church at Nicaea involved itself with no hesitation in the administrative structures of imperial Rome, whose great heritage Constantinople, the 'new Rome', was to take to itself and enrich. So the fifth Canon of Nicaea orders the meeting, twice a year, of an episcopal synod in each *eparchy* (civil province). Between 341 and 381,

a council held at Laodicea, in Phrygia, demonstrates the union con-
summated between civil and ecclesiastical administrations in its
characterization of itself as an assembly of delegates from 'the various
eparchies of Asia' (the fourth civil diocese). One can understand how,
around 340, both Eusebius of Caesarea and Athanasius of Alexandria
can speak of the 'ecumenical' synod of Nicaea: the notion had become
a common one, designating the highest possible level of decisions,
extending over the greatest imaginable jurisdiction, taken in a Church
presided over by the Emperor.

This state 'ecumenicity', added to the need for a degree of orthodoxy
felt by all the bishops of the *Oikoumènè,* also explains the destiny of
the 'faith' that emerged from Nicaea. This confession of faith, even
before the closure of the synod, represented a victory for the 'political
party'. Or rather, since we do not know enough to divide the bishops
into parties of 'politicals' and what might be called 'spirituals', we
should perhaps say that Nicaea placed all the council fathers in a new
situation very different from their previous experiences in the service
of the Churches. The immediate acceptance of the ecumenicity of the
imperial decision forced a new style and unaccustomed procedures on
their debates. Undoubtedly through a certain amount of improvisation,
they learned to exercise the ecclesiastical magisterium in more or less
direct contact with the imperial majesty. This is an explanation for the
form of 'political' compromise eventually taken by the Nicene Creed.

This evolved from the old formulation of baptismal vows, keeping
the essential elements of the formula used by the Church of Caesarea,
whose respected bishop Eusebius was rightly seen as a 'moderate' and
a master of the art of conciliation. This formula was given various
linguistic clarifications designed to decide the dogmatic conflict between the supporters of pro-Arian positions and those opposed to
them. The word *homoousios* ('of one substance'), adopted to define the
divine nature of the Son in relation to that of the Father, is the best
illustration of the *political* nature of the 'faith' declared orthodox at
Nicaea: the word did not belong to the terminology of any of the groups
of opposing theologians; furthermore, it had been avoided till then by
Bishop Alexander of Alexandria in the heat of debate that had been
going on for years; his opponent, the priest Arius, used it only to reject
it as tainted with gnostic anthropomorphism. After Nicaea, Athanasius, who succeeded to the see of Alexandria in 328, spent almost
half a century in tempestuous efforts at defending the 'faith' of Nicaea,
but being careful not to take the too problematical *homoousios* as his
own. By a singular irony of history, this key word, forced on the
fathers of Nicaea by a process historians have not yet succeeded in
puzzling out,[5] was to lend strength to all those who during Constan-

tine's lifetime, but especially during the reign of his son Constans (337–50), were to attack Nicaea as an unwarranted innovation in the tradition of the faith.

When he took the side of these successive waves of anti-Nicene reaction, the Emperor found himself faced with the strict, unyielding Athanasius, first witness among the Eastern bishops to resistance to imperial papism. The State distraint on the Churches, celebrated with a certain thoughtlessness and plenty of euphoria in 325 and the immediate post-conciliar period, was in fact, for tens, hundreds, and perhaps even thousands of years, to drag all official confessions of faith in the wake of top-level political decisions.

## THE DOGMATIC STAKES

### The Judgment of the Magisterium

While the lasting significance of Nicaea 325 in the history of the Church is based on the meeting there of two forms of ecumenicity—the 'ecumenical' strategy of Constantine in politico-religious matters and the 'ecumenical' consciousness informing the synodal life of the Eastern bishoprics—it is still true that the Confession of Faith produced there formed the basis for the traditional ideology of the Churches because of its strictly dogmatic value. The council fathers of 325 enjoyed freedom of choice, according to the few but independent and varied testimonies we have, which allow an echo of their deliberations to filter down to us. This point is of capital importance: it is not a mistake to see the doctrinal choice made at Nicaea as purely ecclesiastical in nature, uninfluenced by the whim of the emperor, despite the truly spectacular political standing of this synodal assembly. This means that the dogma of Nicaea marks a unique moment of the greatest significance in the inner dynamic of the believing traditions, in accordance with the historical rôle each played in the cultural context of the early Church.

This dogma was first a judgment. All episcopal synods charged with examining doctrinal questions have, till the recent past, instituted trials, pronounced verdicts, excluded those they considered 'deviationists' from the ecclesial community and so guaranteed 'orthodoxy' in what they saw as its most legitimate guise. From this point of view, the dogmatic force of the Confession of Faith of 325 is still synonymous with the rejection of the Arian theses. These had already been censured by a synod of Alexandria, in 318 or 319, when Arius and thirteen of his early supporters had been excommunicated. The head of the Egyptian Church, Alexander, had informed his brother bishops of the Christian *Oikoumènè* of this in a synodal letter, as was proper, followed by the signatures of thirty-six priests and forty-four deacons. Another synod, far less well-known, held at Antioch in the winter of 324–25, had reiterated the condemnation of Arius in view of the internationalization of the conflict he had unleashed in the bosom of the Alexandrine community.[6] The originality of Nicaea, which after all passed judgment on a matter already twice decided by the competent authorities, was to have given this judgment, in the shape of a dogma canonized and a heresy condemned, an 'ecumenical' value which called all the Churches to 'normalize', to standardize their doctrinal relationships, at the outset of the Constantinian era.

This 'normalization' of Nicaea had not been dictated by the Emperor as to the content of the 'faith' put forward to the council fathers for their signature. Neither had it been foreseen by any of them in the official form in which they finally ratified it. One of the major paradoxes of this synod is seeing the condemnation of Arius, which could hardly have been other than confirmed, lend itself to a judicial operation in the grand manner, taking even the principal protagonists of the affair by surprise. In fact, the judgment exercised by the synodal magisterium of 325, instead of simply approving what the bishop of Alexandria had already stipulated and what had been sanctioned against Arius at both Alexandria and Antioch, involved an unaccustomed and unexpected procedure: the assembly was invited to express its disapproval of the Arian theses by appending its signature to the baptismal vows of a local Church—in the event that of Caesarea—, but after those vows had had polemical formulae fatal to the cause of those who were to be condemned inserted in them. This 'ecumenical' levelling of a set of baptismal vows, previously venerated as one of the most precious treasures of a particular ancient Christian tradition, seems a good indicator of the combination henceforth accepted in principle between the two forms of ecumenism put into practice at Nicaea. The magisterial judgment, applied by the fathers of 325 on the level of an 'ecumenical' decision, to which the free initiative of the Emperor had raised them, abandoned the locally defined structures in which the relative ideological autarchy and doctrinal steadfastness of the Christian metropolises of the third century had flourished, siding with the imperial style of administrative ecumenicity. Furthermore, the judges of Arius assembled at Nicaea made up an exceedingly disparate assembly; they came from very different societies and cultural levels, and were badly prepared or little inclined to take part in a doctrinal quarrel belonging to the Alexandrians. All these reasons undoubtedly inclined them toward a formula of compromise, which facilitated the task before them, but was to embitter inter-church relations for many a decade to come. The advantage of the formula adopted lay in its being based on the peaceful usage of a consecrated tradition of faith, which could only please the assembled fathers, even if slightly different formulae were in use in their own Churches; the anti-Arian clauses added to the canonical expression of this tradition of faith then appeared as no more than explanations of what the old formula stated.[7]

## The Confession of Faith in the Crisis of the Traditions

Nicaea 325 undoubtedly provided a new style of magisterial judgment, but its existence has a place in the logic of history not explained by the juridical forms of its 'faith'. The synod of Nicaea experienced all the ideological forces at work in the Churches of its time, brought together in confrontation, if not in creative harmony. This gives still another meaning to the ecumenicity of Nicaea, the theatre for establishing the rift between different conceptions of the evangelical faith, which was to undergo a decisive shift in the spiritual status of its faithful as a result of the confrontation of that time. In this respect it is not easy to assess the dogmatic status of the 'faith' promulgated by the fathers of 325. Of course the *homoousios* and the anathema pronounced against the slogans attributed to Arius clearly established the new, polemical sense given to the old articles of a baptismal confession of faith. From then on, orthodoxy would involve rejection of anything that smacked of Arianism. Furthermore, this 'faith' ratified by the highest authorities of the Churches and the State (even though the imperial chancellery certainly did not add its own words, as it was to do at later councils), became the governing norm of Christian teaching on the nature of God. But the properly dogmatic significance of the Confession of faith at Nicaea in the history of Christianity does not end with the anti-Arian injunctions and the excommunications that characterize them, nor with its universal role as canonical norm; Nicaea did not become a pole of ancient dogma merely as a unilateral act of rejection, nor as an act of ideological absolutism of divine right. The Churches needed, for their own health, a summit meeting of this kind. The procedures of the old synodal regime of the third century were no longer adequate to overcome their doctrinal problems. From this point of view, the synod of Nicaea bears the stamp of an evident need for clarification, the urgency of which was, without doubt, felt in the different metropolises of Christendom, but to which none of them could any longer claim the right to provide an adequate response in the name of the others. By functioning at this new level of decision-making, Nicaea provided, if not immediately, then at least by way of reaction in the decades that followed, the *dénouement* needed by all the participants in this huge ideological drama.

Ecclesiastical dogma on God had been handed down through some remarkable achievements in the course of the three preceding centuries. What canonical form would it take in a Christianity in the process of becoming an imperial religion? The anti-Gnostic struggles of the second and third centuries had led to a strengthening of the historical realism of the Gospel, to a thematization in terms of Christian theology of the Jewish dogma of God as creator and saviour, to establishing the juxtaposition and doctrinal harmony of the writings of the Old and New Testaments, and to development of the presbyteral and episcopal structures in the Churches. Matters of a dogmatic nature, like the affair of Sabellius in the Alexandrian community, or Paul of Samosatos at Antioch, had led to declarations in which the greatest centres of Christendom were directly implicated. But no one had ever questioned the instinctive allegiance of the foundations of the old theism of the cosmic religion, practised by the best Christian thinkers of this often secular tradition. Even Christianized by high-flying Alexandrian geniuses such as the generous Clement and the bold Origen, this theism implied a particular view of the Son of God, and therefore of the divine Trinity as taught in terms of the gospel, that ecclesiastical catechesis was ultimately unable to accept. To distinguish the Christian affirmation of a triune God from its theistic expression modelled on the basic tenets of religious Hellenism, was a task that neither Alexander of Alexandria, nor Arius, and certainly not Eusebius of Caesarea or the 'Eusebians' ranged against Alexander in favour of the Arian theses—nor, finally, the bishops of the whole *Oikouménè* assembled at Nicaea—were capable of distancing themselves from sufficiently to appreciate the change taking place and the whole significance of such a basic quest. It is, nevertheless, the achievement of the Council of Nicaea to have declared its 'faith' in the direct line of this change, to the benefit of Christian affirmations about God to this day.

The verdict of history on the dogmatic value of Nicaea 325 would then be this: the crisis of the believing traditions affecting more or less all the Churches of the day was tackled there at its decisive point—the articulation of Christian dogma on the nature of God. The ecumenical significance of the Nicene Confession of Faith cannot then be appreciated as fairly as it should if confined to the immediacy of its condemnation of Arius. It can better be seen, it would seem, in the context of the overall process through which the Spirit constantly guides the Churches toward the novelty of a gospel they have yet to discover.

*Translated by Paul Burns*

## Notes

1. For example, the synod of Elvira, around 300, had 19 bishops and 24 priests; that of Arles, in 314, 33 bishops, with the bishop of Rome being represented by two priests and two deacons; that of Alexandria, in 318, some 100 participants, who excommunicated Arius and his most faithful friends. The exact number of the council fathers at Nicaea is not known; it was probably about 270.

2. H. J. Sieben, 'Zur Entwicklung der Konzilsides' I–II, in *Theologie und Philosophie* 45 (1970), pp. 353–89; 46 (1971), pp. 40–70.

3. 'The last age predicted in the prophecy of Cumes has arrived, all begins anew and a new order of the centuries is born . . . The earth is delivered from everlasting terror. This child will receive the divine life . . .' (Budé Coll., tr. Goelzer, p. 42).

4. C. Andresen, *Die Kirchen der alten Christenheit* (Stuttgart, 1971), II, 3, 'Die "Okumenizität der Bischofskirchen'; compare III, 3, 'Verweltliechung in Organisation and Repräsentation (der reichskatholischen Kirche)'.

5. G. C. Stead, ' "Homoousios" dans la pensée de saint Athanase', in *Politique et Théologie chez Athanase d'Alexandrie,* ed. Kannengiesser (*Théol. Hist.*, 27, Paris, 1974).

6. L. Abramowski, 'Die Synod von Antiochen 324–25 und ihr Symbol', in *Zeitschrift für Kirchengeschichte*, 1975, pp. 356–66.

7. If one remembers the innovations made by Vatican II in the realm of procedure, modifying and creating from scratch, one is better able to understand the successful but precarious novelty of the magisterial judgment initiated at Nicaea. V. P. Levillain, *La mécanique politique de Vatican II* (*Théol. Hist.*, 36, Paris, 1975).

Ronald Modras

# The Functions and Limitations
# of Credal Statements

CREDAL statements serve a variety of functions within Christianity, even as they do in other world religions. The Jewish *Shema* ('Hear, O Israel, the Lord is your God . . .') and the Moslem *Shahadah* ('There is no God but Allah . . .') perform the same or similar rôles as the many different forms used by Christians to say *Credo*.[1] These functions are not always easily distinguished in the concrete, nor are they all equally important. Sometimes they overlap, or one function predominates over the others. All together, though, they indicate that creeds provide a service to Christian faith that is virtually indispensable.

FUNCTIONS

## Confessional

The principal function of credal statements constitutes their essential definition: they are public confessions of faith, open declarations of one's deepest beliefs. There lies in each of us a natural tendency to say aloud that which we hang our hearts on. 'I confess to you, O Lord, that men might hear . . .', Augustine wrote.[2] The confession of faith, like the confession of sins, follows from our nature as social beings. Already in the New Testament the distinction was made between internal faith and its public manifestation. 'For man believes with his heart and

36

so is justified, and he confesses with his lips and so is saved' (Rom. 10:10; cf. also Jn. 12:42).

Credal statements follow too from our nature as intelligent beings. As there is no human existence without thought or language, so too is there no Christian faith without words. Christianity cannot exist mute; from the very beginning Christians have known what they believe and have found words to express what they know. Originally, confession in Christianity referred to the act of confessing one's personal trust in God and Christ, but the word soon came to be applied to the explication of that trust. We cannot repress our cognitive faculties in any realm of human life, including the religious. Methodological thought responds to religious experience with conceptual formulations. These formulations are not identical with revelation; rather, they are part of the human faith response to revelation. Revelation from the beginning was accompanied by theology, by human knowledge, language, and reflection.[3] The conceptualization of faith (*fides qua creditur*) into credal statements (*fides quae creditur*) is an irrepressible human activity. Paul Tillich correctly pointed out that 'a church is not quite consistent when it avoids a statement of faith in terms of a creed and at the same time is unable to avoid expressing the content of its creed in every one of its liturgical and practical acts'.[4] An act of worship is a form of credal statement, and conversely, to confess a credal statement is an act of worship.

## Doxological

Closely related to confession is doxology, the liturgical expression of praise to God. *Confession* in the Septuagint (*homologia*) because of its related compound (*exomologia*), came to be identified with giving thanks and praise. Christians were influenced by the use within Judaism of a number of psalms and the *Shema* as credal prayers. One of the earliest confessional statements in the New Testament, Philippians 2:5–11, has the form of a hymn. Its origin within a worship setting is further indicated by the call for every knee to bend and every tongue confess that Jesus Christ is Lord.[5] The New Testament suggests too that a confession of faith was expected at baptism (Acts 16:30 ff.; 1 Tim. 6:12); this constituted the earliest and most consistent liturgical use of credal statements. The Roman Creed, direct ancestor to the Apostles' Creed, took shape in the second and third centuries in the context of baptism. When questioned as to belief in Father, Son, and Holy Spirit (Mt. 28:19), the person to be baptized would answer *credo* and then be plunged into the water. From this tripartate dialogue came a short Trinitarian formula to which there was later added a fuller account of the significance of Jesus, the decisive and distinguishing factor of Christian faith. Recounting what God has accomplished in Christ constitutes Christian worship in its fullest and purest form. The Eastern Orthodox churches have traditionally seen a close correlation between theology and doxology.[6] *Lex orandi, lex credendi* is a principal with a long history within Roman Catholicism; it can be interpreted both ways: praying is believing and believing is praying. Luther recognized the doxological aspect of credal statements when he compared the Apostles' Creed to the Lord's Prayer. For worship as well as credal confession, the object is the same. 'I believe in God . . .'

## Catechetical

Baptism occasioned not only the liturgical but also the catechetical use of credal statements. Instruction (*catechesis*) was required to prepare adult converts for baptism. St Cyril of Jerusalem refers to the practice of giving catechumens a creed (*traditio symboli*) which they were to commit to memory and then, at the culmination of their prebaptismal formation, reproduce by heart (*redditio symboli*).[7] The major portion of Cyril's *Catechetical Lectures* consists of an exposition of the successive articles of the Jerusalem Creed, which he regarded as serving as a convenient synopsis of Christian faith. Creeds were thus a by-product of the early Church's catechetical system.[8] With the rise of infant baptism, however, and the decline of the adult catechumenate, creeds became useful for teaching not only neophytes. The so-called Athanasian Creed (*Quicunque*) served as a popular vehicle in the Middle Ages for instructing clergy and laity alike.[9]

Bearing upon the catechetical use of creeds is the concept of the canon or rule of faith (*regula fidei*), applied by Irenaeus and Tertullian to summary statements of belief. The term seems to have been used in the East principally to refer to all of sacred Scripture; in the West it referred often to a baptismal confession of faith.[10] Underlying this apparent inconsistency is the relationship between the creed and the fuller apostolic preaching, of which the creed is simply a brief summary or high concentration.[11] Cyril of Jerusalem described the articles of the creed as being chosen from, and established upon, the Bible.[12] For Augustine too the creed served as a *verbum abbreviatum*, a summary for beginners for understanding sacred Scripture.[13] Abbreviative, recapitulating statements of faith have been part of the Church's catechesis from the outset. The early Church Fathers never forgot, though, that creeds were just that—abbreviated summaries, pointing to a fuller rule of faith expounded in the Scriptures.

*Kerygmatic*

The Church confesses its faith not only to its own but to the world. It has continued the mission and ministry of Jesus by proclaiming the Christian message to all who would hear. This proclamation (*kerygma*) has always had the gospel for its object, but a gospel which has taken a variety of forms. For Jesus it meant announcing the kingdom of God. When the Easter-event brought an entirely new set of circumstances, the messenger became the message, and the preaching of the kingdom became the preaching of the Christ. The variety of theologies in the New Testament clearly demonstrates the ability of the Church to accommodate the expression of its message to changing missionary situations. The need did not end with the first century. In 325 the Council of Nicaea found itself compelled to formulate a creed with the use of non-biblical language. There were those at Nicaea who were reluctant to describe Jesus as 'one in being with the Father' (*homoousios*), simply because the term was not found in Scripture. As Athanasius argued, however, the doctrine was biblical, even if the word was not, and the word was necessary to express the doctrine unambiguously.[14] The Nicene Creed was a way of saying that Christian faith can be translated into fourth-century Greek.

Credal statements are interpretations of the Christian message in terms of different historical and cultural circumstances. Such interpretation does not proceed simply from logical deduction but from a living encounter between the gospel and the people living in a particular time and place. An exchange between the gospel and a new existential situation requires a new expression of the Christian message. Whether biblical or conciliar, a credal formulation cannot help but bear the signature of the culture from which it emanated. Language and its conceptual elements are embedded in a particular historical and social fabric.[15] This means that the Christian message must be translated anew regularly if it is to be intelligible and have an impact on people's lives. Formulating a creed, therefore, obviously requires both fidelity and creativity, not only memory but imagination.

*Apologetic*

In turning to the world, the Church needs not only to explain itself but to be 'prepared to make a defence' (*apologia*) to any who call for an account of its hope (1 Pet. 3:15). Credal statements have an apologetic or defensive function, drawing lines of demarcation between its own message and that which is unchristian. Even in the New Testament, basically positive expressions of faith often came to acquire a defensive or polemical pointedness. Paul's affirmation of faith in one God and one Lord (1 Cor. 8: 5–6) bears the distinct ring of a polemic against the polytheism and emperor worship of first century Hellenism. To say that Jesus is Lord was to say that Caesar was not, and martyrs like Polycarp accepted death rather than say *Kyrios Caesar*.[16]

Besides defining what is Christian and what is not, credal statements also draw lines between orthodoxy and heresy. Paul quotes an already existent formula (1 Cor. 15:3–5) against Corinthian Christians who denied the resurrection of the body. The Johannine writings insist that Jesus has come 'in the flesh' (1 Jn. 4:2; 2 Jn. 7) against Docetic Christians who denied Jesus' humanity. The campaign of the Apologists against Gnosticism played an important rôle in shaping credal formulations.[17] Tertullian and Irenaeus reveal a distinct anti-heretical animus in their summaries of faith. When Arius and his followers devised a creed-like summary of their theological position, denying Jesus to be anything more than a creature, Nicaea was compelled to take a stand and to say *no*. Saying *no* is an important and time-honoured function of credal statements. That the need for them continues was proven in 1934, when the Barmen Declaration raised a clarion call to German Protestants for a *yes* to Christ and a *no* to the Nazi Führer. Emergency situations require extraordinary measures, and credal statements are sometimes crisis measures made in self-defence. Their polemical nature should not be viewed as purely negative, however; drawing lines and saying *no* to something is a way of saying *yes* to something else. Polemics are the other side of loyalty.

*Integrative*

Finally, credal statements have an integrative, ecclesial function. They integrate the individual believer into the local church and the local church in the Church universal. Even when spoken in the singular, 'I believe' means 'I believe with the Church and with the faith that brought me into the Church'. Because Christian faith takes place in the Church, it is necessarily a communal concern. The Church is both the hearer and preacher of God's revelation. Witness (*martyria*) is the act of an individual, but confession is essentially the act of a community. This integrative or unifying function of credal statements is expressed by the New Testament term for confession, which retained its classical meaning of agreement or compact (*homo* = common, same + *logia* = word). This aspect of correspondence or agreement is also signified in the term *symbolum*, which came to be applied to the formal creeds of early Christianity. *Symbolum*, originally a token, distinguishing emblem or sign of authenticity, comes from the Greek verb meaning to throw or cast together. The term appears to derive from the custom, popular in antiquity, of breaking a ring or tablet in two; the corresponding pieces would be fitted together as a token of identity for guests, messengers, or partners to a treaty. Thus a credal formula would serve as a symbol or a sign of recognition, permitting individual believers and churches to identify each other as sharing the same faith.

To perform this unifying function, creeds necessarily enjoy a certain normative character. A credal statement constitutes the Church's canonization of a theology. Faith, which depends upon preaching, depends upon language, and the communality of Christian faith requires a certain communality of theological expression. A credal statement represents an authoritative ruling by the Church on terminology: Sprachregelung). This inner-church determination of linguistic usage is necessary for the sake of Christian unity. 'It must be possible to have a theology which is authoritatively binding'.[18]

LIMITATIONS

Following directly from the functions of credal statements, as I have delineated them here, are their unavoidable limitations.

1. Credal statements are confessional: conceptual formulations, theological symbols that point like fingers to the stars. Because they employ a language that is analogical, they are more different from the reality they represent than alike, hiding more than they reveal. Yet we use them, as Augustine said of the word 'person' when applied to the Trinity, 'for the sake of speaking of things that cannot be uttered'.[19] Credal statements stand under the limits of language; this precludes their being undialectically identified with revelation. They do not comprehend the incomprehensible. They do not exhaust the fullness of the mysteries of which they speak. They are not simply the truth of the matter. They are not the best we could say. God is always more. 'Our words are only a stammering before the reality we confess'.[20]

2. Credal statements are doxological: confessions of praise and thanksgiving, worship of a God who suffers no god beside him. Formulated by weak, sinful, fallible human beings, they bear all the marks of weak, sinful, fallible human beings. Even when they are true, they can be 'rash and presumptuous . . . dangerous, equivocal, seductive, forward'.[21] Even when justified, they can be arrogant, unteachable, susceptible of misunderstanding and doctrinaire fossilization.[22] Even when necessary, they can be the product of a drive for power and prestige.[23] Because the human mind is a 'perpetual manufacturer of idols' (Calvin), credal expressions of faith are always in danger of being

made into objects of faith, into infallible sources of security. Credal statements stand under the first commandment and the cross, under the prohibition against idols and the divine judgment against all endeavours to transcend human limitations. Christians believe not in the Bible, not in the teachings of the Church Fathers, not in the pronouncements of popes, but in the God to whom they all attest. Whether biblical or conciliar, credal statements are never above the influence of sin, which affects the human intellect as well as the will. They are not ultimate, not infinite, not divine. 'We believe in one God . . .'

3. *Credal statements are catechetical:* abbreviations for the sake of instruction, summaries taken from Scripture to serve as useful tools for teaching. Because they are selections, they are always selective. Because they are concentrations, they are always reductive. There is much that is missing from the ancient creeds: no mention of Jesus' life, ministry, or preaching, no mention of redemption or reconciliation, baptism or eucharist. Whether ancient or new, because they are parts, they need to be seen in the light of the whole. Ideally brief for use at worship, they are fragments which point to the fuller tradition from which they were taken. Credal statements stand under the canon of Scripture. They were not created *ex nihilo* but from an apostolic preaching handed down in the Bible. They are not the full gospel. They are not the whole tradition. They do not deny that of which they are silent. They are not textbooks of theology but tools for teachers, aids for learners, and we are all learners.

4. *Credal statements are kerygmatic:* interpretations of the Christian message, translations of the gospel for a particular time and place, conditioned by the culture giving rise to them. Under the impact of history, words change their meaning. A dogma or creed formulated in one era can mean something else in another. The Church does not control language. Societal forces change people's questions and concerns, the categories in which they think. Words like salvation and grace can become stale. Concepts like hypostatic union can become ponderous. Time can make credal formulas esoteric and unintelligible, so that their original value diminishes for subsequent generations. Credal statements stand under the 'not yet' of a kingdom and fulfilment still to come. They are not fixed forever. They are not eternally valid or useful, irreformable or absolute. They are not 'superstatements' elevated above the universal law of transitoriness. If they are to communicate a living faith, credal statements have to speak a living language.

5. *Credal statements are apologetic:* defense measures, protections, lines of demarcation. Because they pronounce an undialectical *no* to what is unchristian or heretical, dogmas and creeds often neglect what is valid and human in what they oppose. They can lose the truth of a

half-truth and become one-sided themselves. In defending against error (Arianism), they can so single out one aspect of Christian tradition (Johannine Christology), that other aspects are left undeveloped (the Christology of the Synoptics). In their polemical front against extremes, they can become extremes. Credal statements stand under the amgibuities of our human condition. They are not above the dynamics that govern all social bodies. They do not tell both sides; they do not tell the whole truth. They are not judgments on other people's honesty or integrity, their good faith or good sense. They are crisis measures and not luxuries to be pronounced at will as a proof of authority. They are emergency solutions which should not necessarily be viewed as permanent, lest lines of demarcation harden into schisms.

6. *Credal statements are integrative:* symbols of a common faith, signs of mutual recognition among individual Christians and local churches, binding them together with a language that is binding. Even when the Church says that a theology is normative, however, or that a term is most apt (*transsubstantiation*), it does not thereby prohibit the use of other terminology. The universality of the Church, the inexhaustible potential of its faith for expression, and the historical nature of human culture and language all preclude the monopoly of a single theology. A universal Church requires a plurality of theological expression, and a plurality of theologies leads as a matter of course to a plurality of creeds. To serve as a sign of a common faith, though, any creed in our day would have to be ecumenical, recognized and received as an expression of their faith by the world family of churches. Credal statements stand under the mandate to 'make disciples of all nations' (Mt. 28:19) and become 'all things to all men' (1 Cor. 9:22). This command to be catholic does not permit one credal formula (*ex Patre Filioque*) to eliminate the possibility, validity, or appropriateness of all other formulas (*ex Patre per Filium*). No matter how normative, a creed is not exclusive. To reflect the faith of a universal Church, it may not be narrow. It is not the faith of one man, one local church or one tradition. A catholic faith requires an ecumenical creed.

The functions of credal statements lead inevitably to their limitations, and their limitations lead to the conclusion that, great as they are and as deserving of honour and respect, the credal formulations of the past cannot be expected to achieve in our own day what they did so admirably in their own. Linguistic analysis in philosophy and the historical-critical method in theology have made us more aware than former generations of what creeds can and cannot do. If there is anything else they can do, it is to encourage us in the Church to formulate a creed to meet the crises and challenges of our day, as they did in theirs. If there is something else they cannot do, it is to relieve us of the responsibility to try.

## Notes

1. For the texts of the more important ancient creeds, cf. A. Hahn & G. L. Hahn, *Bibliothek der Symbole und Glaubensregeln der Alten Kirche* (Breslau, [3]1897) (reprinted Hildesheim, 1962).

2. *Confessions*, 10, 3,3.

3. K. Rahner, 'Was Ist Eine Dogmatische Aussage', *Schriften zür Theologie* (Einsiedeln, 1962), 5, pp. 75–79 (English: 'What Is a Dogmatic Statement?' *Theological Investigations*, Baltimore, 1966, 5, pp. 61–64.)

4. *Systematic Theology* (Chicago, 1951–63), pp. 3, 190.

5. V. Neufeld, *The Earliest Christian Confessions* (Grand Rapids, 1963), p. 144.

6. W. Kasper, *Dogma unter dem Wort Gottes* (Mainz, 1965), p. 33.

7. *Catechetical Lectures*, pp. 5, 12.

8. J. N. D. Kelly, *Early Christian Creeds* (London, [3]1972), p. 51.

9. J. N. D. Kelly, *The Anthansian Creed* (London, 1964), pp. 35–51.

10. F. Kattenbusch, *Das Apostolische Symbol* (Leipzig, 1894–1900) (reprinted Hildesheim, 1962), pp. 2, 963.

11. J. Quasten, *Lexikon für Theologie u. Kirche*, 8, cols. 1102–03.

12. Op. cit.

13. *De Fide et Symbolo*, 1,1.

14. *De Decretis Nicaenae Synodi*, P.G. 25, 454.

15. K. Rahner, op. cit., p. 56 (English: p. 44); cf. also B. Sesboüe, 'Autorité du Magistère et vie de foi ecclésiale, *Nouvelle Rev. Theol.* 93 (1971), p. 347; A. Dulles, *The Resilient Church* (New York, 1977), p. 53.

16. *The Martyrdom of St. Polycarp*, 8, 2.

17. J. N. D. Kelly, *Early Christian Creeds*, op. cit., pp. 97–98.

18. K. Rahner, op. cit., p. 65. (English: p. 52.)

19. *De Trinitate*, 7, 4.

20. O.H. Pesch, 'Kirchliche Lehrformulierung und Persönlicher Glaubensvollzug, H. Küng (ed.), *Fehlbar? Eine Bilanz* (Zürich, 1973), p. 273.

21. K. Rahner, op. cit., p. 58. (English: pp. 45–46.)

22. H. Küng, *Infallible? An Inquiry* (New York, 1971), p. 134.

23. O.H. Pesch, op. cit., p. 261.

Kyung Yun Chun

# Confessing and Confession

FROM a remote past, a distinction has been made between *fides quae creditur* and *fides qua creditur*. There seems to have always been a disparity between the traditional, ecclesiastical statement of faith and an actual, personal confessing of faith in a concrete situation. It is noteworthy to see 'the Confessing Community', as the theme of the discussions on reflection on the fifty years of effotts for *consensus* in 'Faith and Order'.[1] The most important task entrusted to the Church by Christ seems to be the proclamation of the Gospel. The order to 'preach the Word, be urgent in season and out of season' (2 Tim: 4:2) and our need 'to make a defence to anyone' call us to account for the hope in us (1 Pet. 3:15); they are statements of the task of Christians in the present world. The Church's work of mission requires an ardent confession of faith from its members. The work of mission was inevitably carried out by denominational Churches, which came to stress their particular experience of faith. In this way, the confession of faith is related to the church mission in a dialectical relationship. Since the International Missionary Council has been integrated into the World Council of Churches, a confessional zeal had been required in the latter more than in the previous stage. Without the resounding voice of confession and a witness from personal conviction of the biblical message, preaching of the Gospel and planned mission can hardly be actualized with strength and authority.

It had been stressed by *Karl Barth* that a confession of faith is an act of the Church and the sole bridge which will connect the Church to the world.[2] The struggle of the German Confessing Church coping with political reality convinced him of this truth. The Church of the present

45

day, harassed by the need to gather together and to promote mutual understanding, does not consider appropriately the meaning of a recital of the confession of the Triune God in unison. The Christian Church is destined to solve various problems in the ecclesiastical, social and political dimensions which seriously concern mankind's survival and spiritual health. While we cope with these problems, we must re-examine all our means of creating confessional relevance. Unless we listen constantly to the words of Christ in the biblical texts, we cannot reach the biblical dimension of faith which alone is able to serve mankind ultimately.

It is my task to analyze and clarify the confessional situation of Christians in their personal, ecclesiastical, social and political dimensions. I shall discuss: confession and discipleship; towards an actual confession; diverse situations of confession and socio-cultural differences; the ecumenical stand of confession and its political dimension.

## CONFESSION AND DISCIPLESHIP

The encounter with Jesus Christ produced a confession and a discipleship. The confession stands in a vertical relationship to the Lord; however the discipleship is horizontal. The first Christians in the lands on non-Christian tradition experienced the call of Jesus Christ as a call for decision for a different way of life. They joined the Christian Church through conversion. It was an adventure which enabled them to transplant to a new community and gave them a new vocation and new world-view. Their faith in God the creator, Christ the redeemer, and the Holy Spirit the sanctifier called them to live at the edge of the world, ushering in an other-worldly reality. Their confession of faith was a motive power which led them to an exodus from their previous life. For the Reformers, the confession of faith was the criterion which discriminated right faith from false; it was their outline of the contents of the Bible according to their understanding of the Gospel. In the present day, we are eager to restore confession as the dynamic power of the discipleship. It is usually said that *credo,* the first word of the Apostles' Creed, is the sole word to indicate a subjective aspect of the confession.[3] The rest of the text designates the objective contents of what one must accept. The faith by which we believe (*fides qua creditur*) becomes a personal conviction. It forms an experience of the Word of God. Life in time is a struggle against temptation and evil powers and can be maintained by this conviction.

Discipleship consists of the call of Christ and response in obedience.

However, the two entities work differently in character. The call operates momentarily and the response works continually. Dietrich Bonhoeffer made a distinction between discipleship and confession.[4] He opined that 'the response of discipleship would be an act of obedience, not a confession of faith in Jesus'. He might have arrived at this view by his overwhelming experience of the confessional movement in his Church. We must acknowledge that there were confessions of faith in the ministry of Jesus before the confession of Peter had taken place. Discipleship started as a recognition of and trust in the person and healing power of Jesus. Jesus healed patients by finding faith in them. The recognition of the divine origin and miracle-working power of Jesus can be extended to a Christological confession. A confessing person can be a disciple with an ever-remaining adherence to Christ. The confessing of faith in discipleship retains a paradoxical character, like that of the father of a paralytic child in the gospel narratives: 'I believe, help my unbelief' (Mk. 9:24). Obedience to the call of Jesus is renewed by a confession of faith.

Confession is cognitive and declarative, but discipleship depends on conviction and decision-making self-surrender. A confession makes the self void, but discipleship makes use of the sinfulness of life. The ultimate citadel which a confession of Jesus has to keep is one that makes open trust in the crucified Christ who justifies the ungodly. Confession alone can prevent the self-righteousness of discipleship as an institutionalized activity of the Church.

## TOWARD AN ACTUAL CONFESSING

Almost everywhere in the East there is to be found the so-called Non-Church Movement. The people of this movement, although a minority, contribute much to an awakening which allows the institutional Churches to reflect on their failure in following Jesus. They positively encourage bible study and grasping of the theme of the Bible. They negate liturgy and the institutionalized Church, and accordingly discard baptism and a confession of faith. Their preference in Bible study is apt to be eclectic. They highly estimate the Pauline Letters and the writings of the Prophets. They actualize discipleship by stressing the autonomous Christian self and creative theological thinking; however they do not acknowledge the necessity of public confession. In the days of persecutions they remained crypto-Christian and did not identify themselves with the sinful Christians who openly confessed Christian faith to the world and remained in the Churches. Although they greatly esteem the vertical relationship of a Christian with biblical revelation, they lose sight of the horizontal solidarity of world-wide Christianity. The basic form of confessing seems to be a confessing of one's sinfulness and at the same time the bounteous grace of God. Without baptism one cannot take part in the solidarity of Christian people and be in line with the saints of the past and the present. A confession means confessing one's own truth perceived by encounter with Jesus Christ.

The distress which is involved in our actual confession of faith is to know the way we relate the confessing of our sinfulness before the grace of Christ to our faith in the Triune God. We must be frank in the judgment of ourselves in the presence of Christ. 'For the Word of God is living and active, sharper than any two-edged sword, piercing to the division of soul and spirit' (Heb. 4:12). We confess our unworthy discipleship as the salt of the earth and the light of the world, and also our failure to take up the burden of the heavy-laden and wearied people of the world. We confess that we could not resist evil and risked bloodshed. We confess that we are not so courageous as to endure contempt and persecution inflicted upon us in the name of Jesus. We regret our pride concerning the success of our Churches in their tight organization and mission. We confess that the love we show forth on earth is not enough to relieve the sufferings of the innocent and tiny souls in our fellow citizens. To confess the faith is to draw a rough outline of the message of the whole Bible. *Karl Barth* taught that the confession of faith is an exposition of the Bible.[5] I found the same in Lutheran confessional writings.[6] How is the statement of our sinfulness in response to the teachings of Christ related to the biblical message? How is the confession related to the exposition of the Bible?

The Bible is not a collection of authoritative fragments, but a collection of writings which have behind them a wholesome history. There is also a consciousness among Christians which may respond continually to the fragmentary address of the words of the Bible in the actual historical situation.

### DIVERSE SITUATIONS OF CONFESSION OF FAITH
### AND SOCIO-CULTURAL DIFFERENCES

Although a Church aims at an outline of the whole message of the Bible in its confession, it is inevitable that diverse sounds are produced by the confessions of the Churches. This diversity grows greater in the cultural and social conditions in which Christians live. In the sixties of the present century, discussions of indigenous Christianity were very active among the younger Churches. Theologians in those Churches

interpreted Christian church history as successive indigenous contribu-
tions of each nation. They interpreted the New Testament as a weaving
of diverse elements of thoughts. They arranged in it Hebraism, Hellenism and Mazdaism, and so on. They expected to learn in the near
future of an easternized interpretation of the biblical message. But
surely a Buddhistic Christ or Shamanized interpretation of the Holy
Spirit is a caricature? Although such an effort would end in a strong
deviation from the biblical message, men in general experience a life of
joy and suffering.

Not a particular finding of religious truth, but a series of human
experiences in general make up this contribution to Christian faith.
These experiences help us to understand the Bible. As the people of the
Old Testament accepted the wisdom of other nations in the ancient
Near East into their Bible, so Jesus Christ raised from the dead makes
use of the general human experience which is deposited in human
spiritual history for a better understanding of the address of the Word
of God. It is said that God gave two books to mankind in order to reveal
himself: the Bible and Life.[7] The confession of faith as an outline of the
biblical message will give order to the multitude of human experiences.
Analogous happenings in nature, in the language of men, become the
vehicle of the message of the kingdom of God. Ancient religious
teachers made good use of the deposit of human experience for
spiritual teachings. The confession of faith does not reject general
human experience but gives order to them. Man can find relief through
his struggle of life and can reach to a higher stage of spiritual maturity.
The confession of faith, however, leads him to meet the Creator, the
Redeemer and the Sanctifier of man.

We are living not in a cosmos, but in a world of many lords and many
gods. The demoniac seems to promote world history. Thucydides
suggested that the initiating motive of history had economic and social
elements. The economic conditions and the character of a political
regime strongly influence the disposition of man. 'Principalities, powers and world rulers of this present darkness' (Eph. 6:12) establish their
own kingdoms and subdue the people for their purpose and usage. The
Christian Church and the Gospel will have nowhere to lay their heads.
However, the confession of faith will take hold of this world and reap
the same fate Jesus was faced with; it will herald the coming of the
kingdom of God. The confessing Church will cling to the last to the
Christ who justifies the ungodly and becomes the Lord of the wearied
and heavy-laden. The confession of faith, holding fast the Christ
Crucified, interprets the given texts of the Bible in its actual historical
situation.

## THE ECUMENICAL STAND OF CONFESSION AND ITS TASK
## IN THE POLITICAL DIMENSION

The historical statements of the confession of faith which have been produced by the Churches are monuments and milestones which indicate the spiritual earnestness of the Churches in their struggle to witness to Jesus Christ. The more precise and sincere the expression of these confessions, the wider the distance which divided one Church from another. Doctrinal precision of creeds hastened a separation of the Churches. While one Church searched after clarification of one truth against falseness of faith, it denounced other Churches as Anti-Christ or heretical. This has been the course of Christianity in the last five hundred years. The ideal of the unity of the Churches has not yet been achieved. Doctrinal diversity has been a great obstacle to the unity of the Church.

Jürgen Moltmann started from the proposition that there were no longer any doctrinal differences which justify the division of our Churches. According to him, theology unites—service divides. Hans Heinrich Wolf, modifying this statement of Moltmann, says: 'Theology unites and leads to agreement, but this agreement can hardly be described as binding'.[8]

'Service, on the other hand, while certainly still directing us, unites, especially in the form of spontaneous church action among Christians of different confessions'.[9] This sounds very optimistic. According to this dictum, ecumenism is not the goal of the discussion of confessional unity, but the starting-point at which we find our common stand in Jesus Christ, as it is expressed in Jesus' farewell address in the Gospel of John (14–16). The ideal state may not be found in the end, but in the beginning. Faith in the Holy Spirit, which is now thought of as essential, favours a diversity of forms of confession. In this dissonance one can listen to the harmonious praise of diverse voices. It is inevitable that we find an answer to a certain doctrinal question in particular denominational articles of faith, whenever Churches discuss with each other. The difference between them should be referred to a belief in the Holy Spirit who will produce a unity in the future.

The Churches now are obliged to analyze and define the nature of man more than to define the Triune God. The Gospel was from the first a call for liberation of man from evil powers, namely sin, disease, poverty, accidental hierarchy of castes, and other binding forces. Modern society dehumanizes men rather than liberates them. The enormous machinery of society which was built by men supplies entities which men cannot escape from or manage. As society grows greater, the Christian Church and the voice of faith become smaller than ever. The Church cannot control secular rulers and Christian truth is not a binding truth on all scientific knowledge. The secular powers, economic and political, have come to hold enormous power; they claim to be gods and saviours of mankind. The Christian Churches seem to be very tiny and insignificant to them. Churches have to pay tribute to the worldly powers and have to maintain themselves in this world. We receive some intimation from the story of Samson as to why he went to the Philistines and behaved as he did; and at last he came to end his life in shame. Also we are not surprised to hear that Abraham, the Patriarch of the People of Israel, pronounced a lie regarding his relation to his wife Sarah in the presence of the trifling pagan ruler of Egypt. Although Christian Churches in the present world acquiesce in the proposal, policy and planning of secular governments, they must witness to the future of mankind in history. The Christian Church must rebuke all kinds of evil which able and wealthy or powerful people have inflicted upon weak and poor people. The Church has to encourage the ruling class or the able to practise justice and loving-kindness to the under-privileged people. In the dictatorial regimes of the present world the evil of rulers amounts to more than we suppose, because they can conceal their evil deeds by their unlimited power; it becomes greater because they disguise themselves as the saviours and benefactors of the people, through the mass media under their control. People under these regimes do not trust the preaching of the Churches on the love of Christ and the bounteous grace of God. The overwhelming strength of the worldly powers obliges the Christian Church to conceal the truth and to suppress a description of facts, and so discard the urgency of God's concern for men from the foreground of witness.

We have to state anew the confessional statement of faith in this rapidly changing world. In the article of the Creator, the magnificent work of God's Creation, the value of human rights and the healing power of nature should be stressed. In the article on the Reconciler, there must be the fact that Jesus Christ was crucified in order to redeem the least of his friends in this world and to restore peace among the people, both the strong and the weak. In the article on the Sanctifier, it should be obvious that the warrant of the future, the Holy Spirit, is sure to replace physical violence and sanctify the ungoldly who live in moral perseverance and in the hope of the consummation of world history through the participation of Christians and secular people. In this way the contents of the confession of faith will reveal the most urgent concern of God to the world.

## EPILOGUE

I have discussed the nature and extent of a present-day confession of faith in our Churches. The confession of faith is not the display of an intellectual solution to the problems which the Church is faced with. It is appropriate to say that 'the Christian faith is not an opinion or a conviction formed by tongue, but an unshakeable trust, an obvious and constant agreement of the heart as very sure comprehension of the truth of God which is described in the Holy Scriptures and in the Apostolic Creed'.[10] It is a confession of its faith in the Triune God in a responsible decision for a discipleship to the Lord in the present course of time. It must be trustful and sincere in its ultimate concern and be faithful to its object, the Triune God, and to men outside the Church. We must orientate our thinking appropriately to the ecumenical age. We are grateful to our Lord that he has given us a fresh impulse to read the Bible as an agent for transforming society. It is our urgent task to devise a fresh outline of the message of the Bible. To this end our discussion of confession has abundant significance for us all.

*Notes*

1. Cf. *Lausanne 1977,* Report of the 50th anniversary meeting of 'Faith and Order', World Council of Churches (Geneva, 1977).

2. Karl Barth, 'Das Bekenntnis der Reformation und Unser Bekennen', *Theologische Fragen und Antworten* (Zollikon, 1957), pp. 257ff.

3. Cf. Karl Barth, *Credo* (Munich, 1935), pp. 5ff.

4. D. Bonhoeffer, *The Cost of Discipleship* (London, 1959), p. 48.

5. K. Barth, *op. cit.,* p. 264.

6. Edmond Schlink, *Theologie der lutherischen Bekenntnisschiften* (Munich, 1946), p. 88ff.

7. Jermias Gotthelf, *Birkhäuser-Ausgabe der Werke Gotthelfs,* Vol. II, p. 70ff. Cf. H. Ott, *Verkündigung und Existenz* (Zürich 1956), pp. 5ff.

8. 'Fünfzig Jahre "Glaube und Kirchenverfassung" 1927–1977. Eine Bilanz ökumenischer Glaubensgespräche', in *Una Sancta* 32 (1977), pp. 245–50, esp. 249.

9. Jürgen Moltmann, 'What kind of Unity?', *Lausanne 77,* op. cit., p. 39. quoted from *The Ecumenical Review,* vol. 29, No. 4 (October 1977), pp. 369ff.

10. *Vierhundert Jahr Confessio Helvetica Posterior,* Akademische Feier, mit Beiträge von Joachem Staedtke u. Gottfried W. Locher (Berne, 1967), p. 23.

# PART II

*What Belongs in a Future Ecumenical Creed?*

# Damaskinos Papandreou

# An Orthodox Answer

A FUTURE ecumenical creed would make most sense if it expressed the unity in faith, that is, the unity of the Church, which is the goal of ecumenism. It would then have binding doctrinal authority because it would not be just the rational creation of the Church as institution, but would, through its spiritual resonance, take its proper doxological place in the life of the Church as a living expression of the common faith.

Although the ancient creeds were historically and culturally determined—they were addressed to the particular people of their time and were concerned with their redemption—they are a guarantee of orthodoxy, an expression of universal validity in the Christian faith, an absolute experience and not just statements of knowledge. This naturally does not mean that the Church does not have the doctrinal authority to work out a new creed if that is called for by the immediate situation. The Church is the locus of the uninterrupted incarnation of truth through the power of the holy Spirit.

The Orthodox Church was not involved in the struggles of the Reformation and Counter-Reformation, and was therefore not forced to work out new creeds or to adopt some sort of Tridentine creed. Nor today, in its preconciliar process, does it see the need for a new creed, or indeed for a discussion of dogmatic issues as such. It believes that it would be useless and perhaps even dangerous to discuss, without compelling reasons, issues which do not threaten the Orthodox Church with heresies and schisms. For, apart from a few dogmatic theologians, there are hardly any of the faithful who feel the need for such a formu-

necessity and justified grounds, to prevent a grave split in the community of the Church or to remove divisions.

As regards an ecumenical creed, I doubt both its possibility and its necessity, for the following reasons:

1. There is no generally accepted, universal teaching authority which could speak with binding force for the whole of Christendom. Such an authority would be conceivable only after the restoration of unity.

2. Even if such a teaching authority did exist, historical experience would point to the impossibility of such a creed. Not even the Roman Catholic Church, with its infallible magisterium and universal ecclesiological structure, has been able to create a new world catechism. It has not found a form of communication suitable for the different individual situations of nations of diverse cultural, social and psychological origin and constitution. Nor is this for lack of attempts: there was an official Tridentine catechism, and Cardinal Gasparri made another attempt more recently, under Pius XI. What holds for a catechism holds equally for an ecumenical creed.

3. Moreover, our serious contemporary situation does not affect a specific Christian doctrine, about which there is doubt, but our common Christian faith as a whole; it is the practice and content of this which is being questioned. In this situation what should any future ecumenical creed, which would have to be short and addressed to all Christians, include and what should it omit? What would be its main elements? Certainly no creed of the ancient, undivided Church says everything that belongs to the faith, nor was that necessary. When the creed is treated as life, its content transcends any definition. Life produces life and the Spirit the letter, never the letter the Spirit or death life. Who can express the incomprehensible and inexpressible mystery of God? Who can define the undefinable without running the risk of turning God into an idol? I do not believe that our present condition can be cured by authoritative definitions. The Second Vatican Council rightly made no attempt of this kind.

4. That is not to say that the Church cannot look for different expressions of the faith to take the message of salvation into the various situations. It would not be useful, but merely comfortable, to seek a unity without diversity to be expressed in a possible common creed. Unity in diversity and diversity in unity characterizes any living Church of Christ, trying to maintain an organic relation to the world and history and giving the truth of the Gospel the flesh of the here and now without affecting its essential continuity. The historical garb assumed by incarnate truth in every period changes nothing of the es-

sence of truth. The drama of the Church is that some of its members can no longer distinguish between essence and form, with the result that they treat formal aspects as essential (the error of traditionalism) or make the central essence relative (the error of misguided reformism).

In my view, the production of an ecumenical creed is not the essential. I now put forward some suggestions about the creed in our ecumenical situation.

(a) We must pay serious attention to the ancient and venerable creeds of the undivided Church, in spite of the frequent claims that they are too remote from our modern intellectual situation. We must investigate the place they have or should have in the life and thought of the Church today. How, today, do we profess Christ as the Lord, the Son of the living God? And how do we transmit this testimony to Christ? Through mere formulas which help the non-theologian to stand up for his faith in its non-Christian environment? To profess our faith today means thinking of the people of today as they really are. And they are the men and women of the scientific and technical age who have lost their bearings and do not know who they are. They seek peace and justice, want to know what contribution Christianity has to make to mankind and world peace. They are the despised and disadvantaged, the people who demand human dignity, the tragically isolated. Our task is the verification of the Christian belief in God, facing the gulf between God and man.

Man wonders whether he should not become part of the content of the statement of faith. What is this 'I' which proclaims 'I believe in one God.'? Why should this 'I' not become part of the creed? Many people claim that man can be included in the creed in the same way as God, Christ and the holy Spirit, but they forget that God's becoming man is inseparably connected with man's becoming man. Too little thought is given to the fact that the whole content of the faith presupposes man and that Christology is essentially soteriology because it bases its legitimacy on an attempt to answer the urgent questions about the nature of man. We often forget that God became man in Christ so that human nature might be shaped by the humanity of God.

(b) Today the creed is bound up with the question of how theology should be done. For the sake of man and the world we should become theologically more faithful, in the sense of a theology which is inseparable from life and doxology and does not try to answer for its content before human reason, a theology which can be harmoniously applied in everyday life. Central to this theology must be the fertile paradox of our faith, the meeting of the horizontal and the vertical which is the originality of Christianity among all religions. It must, in other words, be a theology which can make real for us here and now what we shall experience in the last days, the cohesion of the whole, the harmony of the universe.

If we become more deeply 'theological' in the sense that the service of man cannot be separated from the service of God in worship, our love of God will lead us to our fellow men and our love of our fellow men will lead us to God, and we shall recover the balance between transcendence and immanence.

(c) Only in this way will the separated Christians come to a profession of faith in Christ. In spite of the many testimonies to Christ, which may be determined by time, place and culture, there is only one profession of Christ, just as there is only one indivisible body of Christ. We are on the way towards a creed which will be rediscovered beyond all our divisions, in spite of the different testimonies to Christ, which may even be an enrichment of the one Church. There has not been enough investigation, bilateral or multilateral, to see whether our differences in faith really do divide the Church. Unfortunately there has not been a mutual investigation of the existence of an 'ecclesia extra ecclesiam', which can be recognised in complete fulness where there is unity in the substance of the faith (i.e., the great conciliar creeds) and the basic structure of the Church (i.e., the apostolic succession) is preserved intact.

We therefore have a common task of seeing whether and to what extent the differences between East and West justify a mutual rejection of communication. We must ask ourselves whether our divisions should not be regarded as different forms of the tradition and not divisions in the one tradition of the faith itself. I believe we must also put the question from the other side: not just 'May we have communion with each other?', but also 'Have we the right to refuse each other communion?' Refusal is only right when the essence of faith and Church order compels it. If it takes place without such a compelling reason we incur guilt. If we get so far in awareness, then we can talk about a possible ecumenical creed.

*Translated by Francis McDonagh*

Peder Højen

# A Lutheran Answer

WHEN one thinks about what an eventual future ecumenical creed should contain, one is immediately faced with serious difficulties. There is the question what an ecumenical creed could possibly be if we mean by this in this context a creed which is actual, universal, serves as a basis for the unity of the whole catholic Church and has overcome the multiplicity of all the particular denominational creeds. However, apart from this, there is not only the problem how such a text should be formulated but the far more basic one of how to justify such an enterprise. Must church unity necessarily be reflected in the formulation of such a creed, or are there other ways of expressing it? This question has become the more acute since for many years the ecumenical movement has been trying to solve precisely this problem without so far reaching any practical result.

It is true that here and there there have been 'essential' consensus declarations but where so far some Churches have united the union was in most cases not achieved on this particular basis. A look at today's Christendom shows that a common creed (such as the old Nicene Creed) is no guarantee of church unity, and even in cases where there have been new formulations of credal or quasi-credal texts, these formulae play no decisive part in the life of the Churches concerned. They were either simply not accepted or only accepted in a rather defective state, and so the hoped-for reunion of the Churches did not follow the presentation of such a document.

As we know, a genuine Christian creed comes into being at a moment in time which is charged with a sense of history and truth, a 'kairos' moment (*status confessionis*) but just because of this a *status confessionis* is not established by appointing an ecclesiastical theological commission charged with the drafting of a new ecumenical creed in order to bring about interdenominational reconciliation.

In this context the situation of Churches already involved in reunion or having achieved it is the true *status confessionis* out of which a new creed might arise. It is not the creed which constitutes the condition of a possible church unity but rather the unity of the Church, arrived at in one way or another, which is the condition for the formulation of a new creed. In this sense the 'having united together'—however this has come about—always constitutes the real *status confessionis*.

The attempts at drafting an all-embracing ecumenical creed which could in principle be accepted by all Christian Churches are conditioned by the conviction that it is possible to catch the truth in a fixed, compulsory and verbal formula. This opinion has been seriously questioned in recent years so that from this angle, too, there are grave doubts about the usefulness of such an ecumenical creed. Lutherans who have taken part in ecumenical negotiations have repeatedly stated their confidence that a basis for unity could be found if it could be fixed verbally. But we cannot get round the fact that on this point we have to learn and think again since modern ecumenical trends have come to see that the truth is not simply expressed intellectually in a verbal statement but just as much in the actual behaviour of man.

Numerous recent ecumenical texts constantly link the verbal creed of the Church with its factual credibility as a Church, and at least since the Conference of the World Council of Churches in Uppsala the exposing of ethical heresy has gone hand-in-hand with the finally shattering collapse of trust in a verbal creed as an adequate expression of basic Christian teaching and practice.

An unbridgeable gulf between sharing a theoretical truth and the practical fulfillment of a Christian existence turns the truth of the creed into a lie. On the other hand, truly Christian practice, even if not thought out in detail, allows the inclusion of at least the implicit 'presence' of existing in the truth. Orthodoxy can never stand on its own but must always prove its truth through orthopraxis. The putting of the truth into words always demands the actual doing of the truth. In the light of such considerations it is easy to understand the new appraisal of, particularly the declining value attached to, credal statements while at the same time the insight into the historicity of the Church and of man's existence at large has made the mere repetition of past creeds impossible. The Gospel must always be proclaimed anew in witness and service, not without due consideration for what the Fathers have said, yet first of all with relation to every new historical situation in the corresponding *kairos* of the truth as constantly 'done' again 'in love'. And the feeling grows that such a faith of the 'appropriate time' cannot be contained in words only. The Church's behaviour does not simply accompany the faith as a consequence, but action and verbal expression of the creed are so intertwined that without either the one or the other it is impossible to talk about faith at all.

Finally, it will also depend on the contemporary image of unity how we should judge the justification and fruitfulness of the attempt to arrive at an ecumenical creed. It is possible that in creating an organic union the idea of an overarching creed which has overcome the particular creeds of the uniting Churches may well still appear to be meaningful though not absolutely necessary. But the unity concept of a reconciled diversity through which the united Church consists of denominational Churches, living side by side in reconciliation while at the same time maintaining their specific traditional creeds—an idea recently pursued among Lutherans at the highest level—will imply a far more critical appraisal of an ecumenical creed or it may be considered wholly undesirable. It is of course not unthinkable that such a pluralistic unity might find its new identity in the formulation of a special creed which would nevertheless not be allowed to diminish the claim to validity of the conventional creeds. But this later stage will not exactly help the acceptance of this new special creed which will always be judged or condemned on the basis of its ostensibly lacking present agreement with the contemporary 'mother-creeds' which will always hover over the new formulation of the identity. At the latest in the case of a *status confessionis* this community of reconciled diversity would in any case reach its limit and would break the traditional denominational bonds in the discovery and formulation of the identity which would be implied in this new situation. But then we have precisely the situation mentioned above that a creed will always be the outcome of a historical challenge but never the instrument which will bring about the *kairos*.

If one would therefore vote against the formulation of an ecumenical creed because it is not convincing, the next question is naturally what might then be the pre-condition for church unity. The traditional Lutheran answer is that there is a sufficient basis for unity if there is agreement on the preaching of the Gospel and the administration of the sacraments; in other words, that the Church becomes visibly manifest wherever the community is gathered under the sway of word and sacrament. But this does not really at bottom provide a clear enough definition of the consensus required nor by implication the dissent which it can carry. For what is the criterion by which one will decide ultimately what is the right kind of preaching and which dispensing of the sacraments accords with Scripture? The appeal to the official principle of the Reformation does not solve the problem because there is no unanimity in the understanding of Scripture and both church members and heretics appeal to it. Without doubt it is not merely an aspect but of the essence of Lutheran theology to insist on the solid interlocking of doctrine and unity although this is no longer accepted as obvious in our age. In general, doctrinal differences no longer prevent the practical sharing of the eucharist nor the fact that several denominations— sometimes at the highest level—are serving the secular world hand-in-hand with each other. On the other hand, just because of all this many people wonder why the differences which separate Christians and are constantly brought out should be considered so important when all the other things are obviously possible.

Up till now church authorities and corresponding scholastic theologians have seen a kind of contempt for doctrine in these common activities in the field of worship or charity. But do these common activities not perhaps show that the traditional doctrinal differences have been mainly overcome and that a new, though not yet credally expressed, doctrine has been reached? Because just as a common creed implies a common service of God and man, so does a common witness presuppose a common teaching. The whole credibility of the Church depends on this close connection between doctrine and service. The active confession of the Christian faith may possibly be reflected in a new creed, but it is absolutely certain that an accepted creed without the translation of it into historical fact will remain dead, in so far as Christian truth is concerned. The question of the unity of the Church means for people today mainly the issue of the visibly recognizable notes of the Church in general: how do we recognize the Church of Jesus Christ?

The Church is that 'people of God' which embodies the love and hope made real in word and sacrament according to its specific situation in time and in solidarity with the whole of suffering mankind. Through this embodiment of active love the Church represents a sign of God's truth for all in the world, a pledge of God's presence in the realm of suffering and evil, which will only reach its definitive fulfilment in the end of time, the *eschaton*. The Church is God's existence through the Spirit in the condition of this world: it is *sacramentum mundi,* the salt of the earth. This Church finds its visible unity precisely in the fact that it is this world-shaped suffering existence, drawing its hope from the one, apostolic and catholic faith as it is expressed in the basic formula of the World Council of Churches. Because of this position which obviously has to be constantly re-shaped dogmatically, Christians are called to give concrete expression to their hope in their own contemporary context, and to show precisely in this way the universality of their faith. To bring this out is more important than labouring to achieve an ecumenical creed.

*Translated by Theo Westow*

David Willis

# A Reformed Answer

FIRST, a future ecumenical confession will attest the reality of the Triune God who evokes such a confession.

Surely a confession will have also to deal concretely with contemporary aspects of the human condition, with human rights and entanglements in which men and women are caught on a global scale today. But it dare not do so as if that were the correct starting point for dealing with human glory and tragedy. For it is in the light of the self-disclosure of the Triune God that societal and personal structures are ultimately to be understood and transformed. Such an approach is not an evasion of orthopraxis in favor of orthodoxy. Nor is it a theological positivism which ignores the untold riches of sociological, psychological, political-scientific, economic-historical resources for analyzing and influencing human conditions. It is simply an insistence that one thing to which a future ecumenical confession must hold is the priority of God's revelatory, delivering and reconciling activity. Such a confession therefore involves a renunciation of those reductionist tendencies which are merely anthropological theologies of glory or despair insofar as they choose to get on with the business of religion, human potential, or political renewal, treating God as an afterthought or as a euphemism for subjective projection.

Put positively, this affirms the transcending freedom of God to be for himself and therefore to be for his creation. Acknowledging God's transcendence demands restatement and reinterpretation, not abandonment or mere repetition. The Reformed tradition has made much of this by using such categories as the sovereignty of God, the majesty of God, the glory of God, the doctrine of justification by grace alone through faith, and the prevenience of grace in the transformation of culture. By meeting us, God makes us to experience transcendence; yet in his free movement towards us he remains the sovereign partner in that encounter and is never restricted to the experience which his freedom creates.

For the knowledge of this transforming self-disclosure, the Church is as dependent today as ever on the history of God's covenantal dealings with the people whose lives make up the stories of the Old and New Testaments. Any future confession of faith must reassert the normative character of the canonical Scriptures in our knowledge of God and knowledge of self. It must, however, do so by registering the advances made beyond the ways Scripture and tradition have often in the past been polemically counterbalanced or treated as competing sources of revelation. The radically different cultural settings behind the texts are not incidental to the weight Scriptures have for the Church: part of what is normative is the process in which the fidelity of God is counted on under remarkably diverse conditions. In making and remaking the canonizing decision, the Church is proclaiming its faith that there is an unfolding economy of God, a discernible purpose of promise and fulfillment which leads up to, is contained in and extends beyond the life, death and resurrection of Jesus Christ.

The Church's confidence in the diversity and unity of revelation is grounded in the nature of God who stands behind his Word. The doctrine of the Trinity is an essential part of the Church's doxological, doctrinal, and ethical participation in the life of the Triune God. A confession of the faith today must insist on the inherently Trinitarian character of the believing community's worship, teaching, corporate life, and worldly witness. This is necessary so that when reference is made to God, it is understood not to mean deity in general but to the one Creator, Deliverer, Sanctifier whom we know in Christ by the power of his Word and Spirit.

Second, a future ecumenical confession will affirm that the presently active Lord over Church and world is the risen Lord, Jesus Christ, the eternal Word of God incarnate, fully God, fully human.

The doctrine of the incarnation will be vigorously maintained over against any tendency to consider it an obstacle to Christian apologetics and religious pluralism. The Chalcedonian decision is as necessary for the Church today as it was in the fifth century, and for the same reasons: humanity's hope depends now as then on the reality of God's taking on our condition in the obedience, death and resurrection of Jesus Christ. To paraphrase Gregory of Nazianzus, because God has assumed the totality of our lives, no corner of them is left without the judging, freeing and reconciling presence of the Word made flesh. It is true that terms like nature and personal (in the sense of hypostatic) have limited usefulness today as they carry overtones of an anachronistic physics. Yet they ought to be maintained alongside more dynamic and relational vocabulary rather than be discarded; for, as Calvin noted in the sixteenth-century anti-Trinitarian debates, the loss or rejection these terms offer covers the rejection of the reality they were intended to express. There are different models by which faith seeks understanding of this mystery, and response to this mystery will continue to take on new language and new thought-forms; but the process of indigenizing incarnational theology takes place precisely because Jesus Christ, the eternal Word of God, makes himself the subject of human words and thought-forms in different cultures and generations.

Third, a future ecumenical confession of faith will attest to the liberating work of the Holy Spirit in the world and Church today.

This is not a shift to something other than a trinitarian or Christological statement; this is about the presence and work of the Triune God through his activity as the Spirit, identifiable ultimately by testimony to Christ and edification of his body, but ever at work in movements beyond the boundaries of the believing community. This pneumatological dimension to a confession is necessarily a part of affirming God's strategy in bringing about the promises contained in biblical visions of justice, and in doing so apparently as often as not through secular and overtly atheistic forces. Of course, there are no grounds here for a spiritual, enthusiastic romanticism about these forces; they they are no more exempt from judgment than religious forces. From the Reformed perspective, however, the doctrine of providence contains within it a necessary note of repentance, a note that the Church cannot triumphantly consider itself exempt from God's rectifying and gracious judgment.

A future ecumenical confession must not be so somber about the structures of evil in the Church and world that it takes the weight of sin more seriously than it takes the victory of grace. It must acknowledge the ways God is at work breaking down barriers between races, sexes, and classes as much in the Church as outside. That is, it must acknowledge God's work through the ecumenical movement of the modern era. God has led the Church into a new understanding and practice of world-wide mission in which the distinction between the so-called sending and recipient Churches has broken down and in which all Christians experience their solidarity and interdependence. Biblical, patristic and Reformation scholarship has resulted in fundamental realignments and convergences on some historically divisive doctrines, such as ministry and eucharist.

The preponderance of ecumenical dialogue is towards recognizing:

that the ministry of the Church is grounded in a mission of the Triune God towards his creation, that the ministry of Christ belongs to the whole people of God, that there is a special ministry of the word and sacrament ordained for the equipment of the saints, that this implies a succession of apostolic message which thus far has itself implied a certain continuity of cultic validation by the imposition of hands and the invocation of the Holy Spirit—and, furthermore, that there are certain loci of this apostolic continuity which have both the power and accountability to exercise the office of teaching magisterium in representative and collegial ways.

The preponderance of ecumenical dialogue is also towards profound re-examination of sterotyped positions on the eucharist. There is a willingness to read with ecumenical perspective the texts of our respective forebearers and to weigh the political, economic and sociological factors which often sharpened divisions among Christians in the sixteenth and subsequent centuries. A future ecumenical confession must attest to Christ's Real Presence in the Lord's Supper, his active use of the *anamnesis* of the community in that act, his re-presentation in the eucharist of his sacrifice made once-for-all, the use of the *epiklesis* in the consecration of the elements, and Christ's joining the faithful to himself by the power of the Spirit in this foretaste of the eschatological banquet.

Oliver Tomkins

# An Anglican Answer

EVERY creed has a history and a context and evokes a response. Unless we are engaging in pure fantasy, this would be equally true of any 'prospective ecumenical creed'. Part of its history would be not only the considerations of earlier essays in this volume but the history of the attitudes to the creeds in those confessions or ecclesial communions from which the 'oikoumene' must grow; part of its context would be how those confessions have viewed each other; part of its response would be the way in which the historic creeds evoke varied confessional response. This essay is an Anglican answer in those three areas.

The reformed Catholicism which became the Church of England in the sixteenth century had, by the nineteenth century, become a loose confederation of autocephalous churches which needed a common forum. Thus in 1867 the first Lambeth Conference was held (the first in a roughly decennial series of which the eleventh was held in August 1978). The Conferences claim no canonical or juridical authority: for that their resolutions need to be adopted by each Anglican Church (today numbering 25) separately. But they have considerable moral authority. So when the third Conference in 1888 adopted 'the Lambeth Quadrilateral' it set a standard from which the Anglican Communion has never departed—and it did so in the context of ecumenism.

The Conference of 1878 had appointed a committee to consider the basis upon which the union of Anglican with other Churches might be considered. The Episcopal Church in the USA in 1886 at Chicago, had already evolved a four-point declaration. Following that lead, the 1888 Lambeth Conference defined the basis as being '(a) The Holy Scriptures of the Old and New Testaments as "containing all things necessary to salvation'? and as being the rule and ultimate standard of faith. (b) The Apostles' Creed as the Baptismal Symbol; and the Nicene Creed as the sufficient statement of the Christian faith. (c) The two sacraments ordained by Christ Himself—Baptism and the Supper of the Lord—ministered with unfailing use of Christ's words of Institution, and of the elements ordained by him. (d) The Historic Episcopate, locally adapted in the methods of its administration to the varying needs of the nations and peoples called of God into the Unity of His Church.' From that day to this, whenever Anglicans have discussed 'the nature of the unity we seek', whenever we have sought 'to give our account of the hope that is in us' for the visible unity of the Church, we have spoken of the Scriptures and the ancient creeds, of the two dominical sacraments and the episcopate as one of the orders of ministry. This four-fold cord is itself spun from strands drawn from varied parts of the life of Anglicanism and especially from the Book of Common Prayer and from the Ordinal and from such historic confessional documents as the Thirty-Nine Articles of Religion (finalized in England in 1571), and as the autonomous Churches developed their own variations of those doctrinal norms. Anglicanism has always laid less stress upon the 'subordinate standards' than upon the primary standards of Scripture and the Apostles' and Nicene Creeds. In England assent to the Thirty-Nine Articles was however for many generations a test for holding any office in the Church (and indeed for admission to the older universities). A less rigorous attitude was adopted in the midnineteenth century and more recently still (since 1975), the admission to office in the Church of England is prefaced by a declaration that, as 'part of the one, holy, catholic and apostolic Church, worshipping the one true God, Father, Son and Holy Spirit', the Church of England 'professes the faith uniquely revealed in the Holy Scriptures and set forth in the catholic creeds, which faith the Church is called upon to proclaim afresh in each generation. Led by the Holy Spirit, it has borne witness to Christian truth in its historic formularies' (viz. the Articles, Prayer Book and Ordinal). The candidate is then asked: 'In the declaration you are about to make will you affirm your loyalty to this inheritance of faith as your inspiration and guidance under God in bringing the grace and truth of Christ to this generation and making him known to those in your care?' The priest then replies to the effect that it is in this context and spirit that he accepts his new office. This awareness that all formulations of faith are historically conditioned documents pervades many recent statements. For example, a comparison between the Lambeth Quadrilateral, 1888, and the way in which the same area was covered by the Lambeth Conference of 1968 shows the same awareness. The attitude of Lambeth 1888 was, as it were, to erect the four walls within which any conversation about re-union must be conducted. The attitude in 1968 was more ambivalent: 'The Quadrilateral has served in part as an indication of those gifts of God to the Anglican Communion which it has received as a part of the one, holy, catholic and apostolic Church and also in part as an indication of what God is calling the whole Church in history more fully to become'. Thus all the marks of the Church are to be seen *both* as gift and as demand, so that with regard to the creeds, 'we, gratefully recognize that the Church in the first centuries gave, to some basic questions implicit in Scripture, authoritative answers which are common ground. We also reognize that our generation is called to live in an epoch when "the faith once delivered to the saints" must be re-interpreted in a form which no part of the Church could accomplish in isolation'. (*Report of the 1968 Lambeth Conference*, pp. 123–4.) A more explicit analysis of the relation between believing and the verbal formulation of beliefs was made in a report by the Doctrine Commission of the Church of England. (*Christian Believing—the Nature of the Christian Faith and its expression in Holy Scripture and Creeds*, London, 1976.) It distinguishes four attitudes to the Creeds in fact to be found among Christian believers; they may be seen as:

(a) norms of Christian belief, not to be replaced by any other formulations since it is by them that new thought-forms and assertions must be measured and tested:

(b) as authoritative statements of the faith of the Church as a whole, but allowing individual reservations about the adequacy of this or that particular affirmation, e.g., of the Virgin Birth, without ceasing to be loyal to the total Church of which creeds are the corporate testimony:

(c) as culturally conditioned statements, adequate to the language and thought of their own time but not so much containing the 'answers' as reminding us of the questions we still need to ask:

(d) as not only historically conditioned but also as inadequate attempts, then as well as now, to capture an always uncapturable infinity of truth; loyalty is always not to the formulations but to the living God whom they attempt, always inadequately, to describe.

The Commission went on to affirm that each, of these attitudes has a place within the dynamic and costly dialogue which must always continue within the Household of Faith.

So, it may be that an Anglican answer to what belongs in an ecumenical creed would be that the classical, primitive creeds can not be discarded but that their *content* is always in some sense relative and conditional—And that for a two-fold reason:

1. Every generation of Christians is always heir to the common history of the Church, in which faith in God has been continuously but variously expressed. This inheritance of faith remains our 'inspiration and direction under God for bringing to light the truth of Christ and making him known to this generation'.

2. Every generation of Christians lives under the eschatological 'not yet'. All aspects of the life of the Church in history partake of this mixture of gift and promise. Yet the relation of the eschatological to the historical is always an imperative. The fact that no formulation of the truth as it is in Christ will ever be adequate is no reason for ceasing to speak as truly as we can. As St Augustine remarked, when we speak of the Three Persons of the Trinity, it is 'not because the phrases are adequate—they are only an alternative to silence'.

Any 'prospective ecumenical creed' would need to start from the classical and primitive testimony to the truth enshrined in Scripture. But because the *Oikoumènè,* whenever and however it comes, will still be subject to the conditioning of history and of the culture of its own time, and will still live under the eschatological 'not yet', it will still be on the voyage of discovery, on the journey from the Christ who has come towards the Christ who is yet to come, held together by his Spirit in a dynamic and costly dialogue. In that dialogue, relationships will often be strained—and in the past they were strained to breaking point. Yet creeds best serve their purpose when they are known not so much as intellectual exercises but as hymns of praise to the Love at the heart of all things, the God whom we must try to describe but only better to worship Him.

Orlando Costas

# A Free Church Answer

THE Free Church response is bound to be least predictable of all those given to the question posed. While the Free Churches are undoubtedly a Protestant phenomenon, the variety of the Churches associated with the tradition makes a definitive and complete response impossible. What follows, therefore, is one response from one adherent to this tradition, one who reads it according to his own ecclesio-cultural experience and historico-cultural situation.

Much of what we mean by the expression 'Free Church' depends on the context. In *Europe,* for instance, the Free Churches are traditionally those that have existed on the fringes of the established or national Churches. They are free because they do not conform to the ecclesial practice of the dominant Church(es), nor accept their theology as normative for the confessions of faith of which they are made up, nor maintain any formal relationship with the State.

When they reached *North America,* however, all the European Churches became free by virtue of the fact that in the new continent the concept of an established or national Church was rejected. The nomenclature was retained, though, to distinguish those Churches not ruled by an historical confession of faith, a common liturgy and ecclesiastical discipline, but which stress the freedom of each congregation to decide its own affairs, reject the institutional and sacramental character of the Church and affirm its communitary, missionary nature.

With the growth of modern missionary endeavour, these characteristics came to identify a significant number of Protestant Churches in what is now called the third world. The new historical situation of the countries it comprises is giving a new dimension to the Free Church tradition. 'Free' in this situation means not only those Churches that preserve the traditional principles of the Free Churches, but also those that commit themselves to the struggles and hopes of the peoples they serve, without expecting political, economic or social advantage from doing so, and without losing their prophetic, critical witness or Christian identity.

## THE ESSENCE OF THE FREE TRADITION

Theologically, there are certain indispensable elements that make up the Free tradition, and must be included in any ecumenical confession of faith. These are, in my view:

### Faith in the Trinity

Faith in the trinitarian doctrine of the nature of God would be a first essential element for the Free Churches. This does not mean that there must be an accepted abstract formulation of this teaching; it means rather that the Free tradition clings to faith in God *as* loving and all-powerful Father, in Jesus *as* beloved and obedient Son, and in the Spirit *as* the presence of the risen Jesus in history, especially (though not exclusively) in the community of faith. The Free Churches have derived their most precious distinctive characteristics from this faith in the trinitarian nature of God. Their traditional resistance to political authoritarianism and ecclesiastical uniformity, and their struggle for freedom of conscience and separation of Church and State, stem from their faith in God as sovereign creator and upholder of the world, giver of life and father of Our Lord Jesus Christ, to whom he has entrusted all power and authority. Faith in the Son has led the Free Churches to stress the command and missionary nature of the Church; faith in the Spirit has endowed the local congregation with all the necessary gifts to carry out its mission faithfully—if the Spirit is with the community, it has no need of ecclesiastical uniformity. For the Free Churches, the Spirit present in the *community* of faith is the principle of Church unity, not the institutional coherence and historical continuity of an ecclesiastical organization.

## The Authority of the Bible

A confession of ecumenical faith would also have to contain a clear reference to the authority of the Bible. By this I do not mean a blind biblicism, but a recognition of the priority given by the Free Churches to the gospel over the Church, and revelation over institutional forms. I also mean recognition of the understanding the Free Churches have of the Bible as the mediation *par excellence* of the Word of God through the written testimony of the prophets and the apostles. Historically, the Free Churches have sought to remain faithful to the theological legacy, simplicity of worship, spiritual warmth and missionary vitality of the early Church as it is sketched in the Scriptures.

This is why, despite the distance between the biblical text and our situation today with its new critical theological problems, going back to its pages, studying its authors and struggling to understand their teachings must be an essential part of an ecumenical confession of faith for the Free Churches. This is because they are convinced that the Bible leads back to the common roots of faith, exists as an objective norm by which to judge how faithful the different traditions are to the gospel, sheds light on the quest for new forms in which the Churches can come together, and is able to provide new solutions to old problems.


## Personal Experience of Faith

The third essential constituent for the Free Churches would be a stress on the personal, experiential dimension of faith. They see faith as not merely *fides* (right doctrine), but *fiducia,* personal trust in the mercy of God through Jesus Christ. They maintain, furthermore, that *fiducia* is not only an instrument for gaining God's grace, but the means to a new experience, the new birth, whose effect can be seen most clearly in a change of life-style with the concomitant gifts of the Spirit and the works of mercy that should accompany it.

This is why they insist that the Church is a community of believing adults. It is not so much personal experience that the Free Churches consider indispensable as the need for conversion as a *sine qua non* for being a member of the Church in its concrete embodiment as *local Church.* This is the ecumenical *crux* for the Free Churches: an ecumenical confession of faith must, for them, find a formula for preserving personal conversion as a basic reference in the historical identity of the Church.

## The Church as Congregation and Mission

This idea, too, is essential to the Free Churches: the Church, they claim, is not distinguished so much by its institutional character as by the fact of its being a congregation of believers. It exists not as an organizational model but as a community in mission. They conceive of the Church as both convocation (*ecclesia*) and dispersal (*diaspora*); a base-community in which what is professed is put into practice and what is practised is proclaimed. This vision requires commitment as a mark of the Church and poses ecumenicity as a question of *praxis,* in the realm not of *being* but of *doing.* Any confession of an ecumenical faith must then take the specific community of the faithful in mission as the essential embodiment of the Church if it is to win the enthusiastic participation of the Free Churches.

## Historical Commitment

Just as it is impossible to discuss ecumenicity outside its specific ecclesio-missionary embodiment, so it is equally impossible to confess faith in the abstract, abstracted from its historical situation, still less without commitment to this situation. So an ecumenical confession would only be possible to the degree that there exists a common commitment to the transformation of the common situation facing our planet. This situation is clearly definable: poverty, exploitation, pollution, alienation, dependency and oppression, colonialism and neo-colonialism. The commitment to transformation is equally clear: socio-political liberation, dignity for individuals and societies, environmental health. There could be no genuine ecumenical confession without a true commitment to the struggle for a juster, more peaceful and healthier world.

### THE FREE TRADITION APPROACH TO A CONFESSION OF FAITH: THE PACT

The foregoing explains why the commonest model of confession of faith in the Free tradition is the pact. Far from being a compendium of theological definitions, the pact, for the Free Churches, has been an *affirmation of faith and commitment* through which union of believers among themselves and with Christ is expressed, by entering into a solemn covenant in which all publicly commit themselves to live the faith they profess and to carry out the mission entrusted to them.

In the situation confronting the world, and in the face of such fragmentation of confessions as now exists, a covenant setting out the basic tenets of the Christian faith in the light of the most pressing problems affecting our planet and committing the Churches to fight to solve these problems, would give a new impetus to ecumenicity. It would in fact place the ecumenical Church in the vanguard of history, which is where it should be but is not, and would free it from the a-historical confessional abstractions in which most of the ecumenical endeavours of our time have lamentably foundered.

*Translated by Paul Burns*

Avery Dulles

# A Catholic Answer

FROM a Roman Catholic point of view, what are the desiderata for an ecumenical confession of faith? What would be its basic characteristics, its structure, and its principal contents? These are the questions to be addressed in the present article.

The traditional creeds and confessions have been, at least in some measure, polemically oriented, whether against pagan errors such as polytheism and emperor worship or against Christian heresies such as Docetism and Arianism. But as the rejected positions lost ground, certain ancient creeds came to be called 'ecumenical'. In recent centuries all major Christian communities have accepted the Nicene-Constantinopolitan Creed, although the Orthodox reject the interpolated *filioque* clause. Although the Apostles' Creed is current only in the West, its teaching is acceptable to the Christian Churches of the East.

The ancient creeds, with their rhythmic articulation and their rich biblical overtones, still possess undeniable power. By their antiquity they communicate a sense of solidarity with the faith of the Apostles and of the Fathers. In their contents, they accent what by a modern reckoning are the principal truths concerning God himself and the mysteries of our redemption. Their attribution of the works of creation, redemption, and sanctification respectively to the three divine Persons continues to inspire modern worship and theology.

Drawing upon the Bible and the ancient creeds, many churches, private groups, and individuals have tried to compose additional creeds and confessions specially suited to our times.[1] These new statements of

77

faith, for the most part, are ecumenical, in the sense that they bypass the issues that divide the Churches and denominations from one another.[2] Some of the recent confessions, however, are divisive in other ways, inasmuch as they embody racial, national, or political concerns not shared by all Christians.

As yet there has been no effort on the part of mutually divided Churches to compose a new creed for our times. If one were composed, it could scarcely be intended to replace the ancient creeds, which still serve satisfactorily as ecumenical norms for doctrine, catechesis, and worship. A new creed, however, could state the Christian message in a more contemporary idiom and relate it more closely to the experience of the faithful today. In form, such a creed would presumably be less dogmatic and liturgical, more personal and reflective, for it is chiefly in personal reflection that the modern religious consciousness unfolds.

While seeking contemporary relevance, a new creed should be designed to challenge the general assumptions of the prevailing culture. It will have an educative function, shaping and not simply mirroring the experience of Christians today. Far from capitulating to current ideologies, the creed will help to offset modern temptations such as hedonism, pessimism, skepticism, and religious relativism.

As regards content, a contemporary creed, as I have already suggested, might suitably adhere to the Trinitarian and Christological emphasis of the ancient creeds and to their accent on salvation history. This dual orientation will have ecumenical value. The Trinitarian and incarnational theme will serve as a bond of the Orthodox tradition, while the theme of salvation history will be appealing to Western Christianity—perhaps especially as represented by Protestantism. These two emphases, however, are not antithetical, since both are integral to the one and indivisible mystery of salvation. In an earlier age, more inclined to metaphysics, it may have seemed acceptable to present the mystery of salvation in abstract and non-historical categories, but in our day it seems fitting to restore the dynamic Pauline understanding of the 'mystery' as God's operative presence in history, especially in Jesus Christ and in the Church. As was noted at Vatican II, the 'mystery of salvation' is the very heart of Christian faith.[3]

An ecumenical confession, by definition, could not affirm the distinctive positions of any one tradition or denomination. From the Catholic point of view, this principle dictates the omission of the modern doctrines of papal primacy and infallibility as well as the particular doctrines defined by popes and councils apart from, or in opposition to, the Orthodox or the Protestants. Actually there is little temptation to in-

clude such modern Catholic developments. According to the common
estimation, the most central religious convictions of Catholics—those
that rank highest in the so-called 'hierarchy of truths'—are rather the
beliefs expressed in the New Testament and in the ancient creeds. As
was noted at Vatican II, these principal articles of faith are shared by
all major Christian groups,[4] and thus afford a basis for joint Christian
witness before the world.[5]

An ecumenical creed, while reflecting what is ancient and common,
could advantageously draw upon the specific insights of particular traditions, such as, for example, the kerygmatic and ethical concerns
characteristic of the Reformation Churches and the attention to the
Holy Spirit and to the liturgy prominent in Eastern Christianity. A
Roman Catholic, making suggestions for an ecumenical creed, will ask
himself what themes and emphases, without being exclusively proper
to his own tradition, may represent the specific contribution which that
tradition may hold in trust for the *Oikouménè*. The following themes,
principally ecclesiological, come to mind:

1. The Church as 'sacrament' or efficacious sign of Christ and of
   the world's redemption.
2. The Church as apostolic—i.e., as perpetuating the authoritative
   testimony of the apostles.
3. The Church as a world-wide communion of faith and charity.
4. The eucharist as the centre of the Church's life of worship.
5. Mary as humanly cooperating in God's redemptive action (and
   thus as type of the Church).

The first three of these five themes reflect the conviction that Christian faith and life are essentially ecclesial. The idea of the Church as
sacrament, although it has firm roots in the patristic tradition, emerged
into explicit consciousness rather recently, and first appeared in official
documents at the Second Vatican Council. The apostolicity and
catholicity of the Church, already affirmed in the Constantinopolitan
creed, are here rephrased with a modern emphasis.

In contrast to baptism, which is commonly referred to in the ancient
creeds, the Eucharist, for some reason, receives no explicit mention
either there [6] or, indeed, in most contemporary confessions of faith.
Yet this sacrament is so central to the Catholic consciousness that it too
would seem to deserve special mention in a contemporary creed.

Reference to Mary is notably absent in most of the contemporary
confessions, even those composed by Roman Catholics. Could this be
in part a reaction against certain exaggerations in post-Tridentine

Mariology? By way of contrast, the true motherhood of Mary was affirmed against Docetism in the earliest creeds, and her divine maternity was explicitly defined, in opposition to Nestorius, by the Council of Ephesus (431). Express mention of Mary supplies concreteness to the theme of incarnation and points up the wonderful manner in which God enables human persons, especially in this uniquely privileged instance, to contribute to the work of salvation.

Because many splendid confessions of faith, thoroughly ecumenical in spirit, have been composed by Catholics in the past decade, I hesitate to add yet another. But, responding to the invitation of the editors, and with a view of illustrating the principles already set forth, I take the risk of submitting the following creed as a sample:

> We believe that the whole world, although scarred by evil and sin, is the work of the one true God, who continues to sustain it and lead it to the goal he intends.
>
> We believe that God has blessed the world by the presence of Jesus, his Son and Mary's Son, who has shown the way to salvation through suffering and love.
>
> We believe that Jesus Christ as risen Lord continues his saving action through the Holy Spirit, abundantly poured forth upon the apostles who were with Peter.
>
> We believe that the Church, under the direction of apostolic leaders, brings together believers of every land as a sign and anticipation of God's coming kingdom.
>
> We believe that all baptized believers are called to share in the tasks God commits to the Church and to partake of the living Christ in the eucharistic meal.
>
> We believe that to all who accept his offer of pardon and who answer his call to loving service, proclaimed through Christ and the Church, God promises eternal life with the saints in glory. Amen.

## Notes

1. Examples in R. Bleistein, *Kurzformel des Glaubens* (Würzburg, n.d.), also the 'Affirmations of Hope' collected in *Uniting in Hope: Faith and Order, Accra, 1974* (Faith and Order Paper 72) (Geneva, 1975), pp. 48–80.

2. An exception would be Paul VI's 'Credo of the People of God' (1968).

3. According to a *modus* accepted by the Secretariat for Promoting Christian Unity, the importance of revealed truths depends on 'their connection with the

history of salvation and the mystery of Christ'. See *Acta synodalia Concilii Vaticani* II, vol. 3, pars. VII (Vatican City, 1973), p. 419, *modus* 49.

4. The ecumenical consensus regarding the principal articles of faith was stressed by A. Pangrazio, 'The Mystery of the History of the Church', in H. Küng and others, eds., *Council Speeches of Vatican II* (Glen Rock, N.J., 1964), pp. 188–92 (*Konzilsreden,* Einsiedeln, 1964).

5. Vatican II, *Decree on Ecumenism,* nos. 10–11.

6. The *communio sanctorum* in the Apostles' Creed was sometimes interpreted as referring to the Eucharist, but this interpretation appears to be secondary and derivative. See J. N. D. Kelly, *Early Christian Creeds* (New York & London, [3]1972), p. 394.

# PART III

*New Ways*

Henk van der Linde

# New Creeds

## CREEDS IN THE MELTING-POT

SINCE 1945, but particularly after 1960, a spiritual revolution took place in the West, of which Christianity, too, still shows the traces. It reached a new way of living the faith which found expression in new patterns embodying the Church, new hymns and songs, and new ways of saying grace at meals. It also found expression in new forms and contents of professing the faith as a statement of belief and of the believer's position in the world. One could no longer understand how to fit the contemporary situation into the context of old symbols and creeds. And so people tried to find new ways and new words to express on the one hand the need and bewilderment, on the other the hope and the promise of our time.

These confessions of faith which originated mainly where young people had their own services or in alternative forms of worship should not be simply identified with the call for a 'brief formula of the faith', as first launched and initially sketched by Karl Rahner.[1] For him, it was first a matter for Catholics because among them, more than anywhere else, the faith had become so overgrown with a layer of centuries-old traditional explanation, as with ivy, that one could hardly recognize the underlying stone structure of the original intent of the revelation. It should indeed be possible in a century of unbelief to tell outsiders briefly and intelligibly in contemporary language what the Christian faith stands for in order to open the way for new questioning and for a new initiation into the faith. He therefore asked for simplicity without simplification by concentrating afresh on the essential. The purpose of the 'brief formula' is primarily missionary but it may also lead the believer to prayer and fresh inspiration. This need seemed to appeal mostly to theologians. It provoked a wave of reaction and of imitation. As far as we know this proposal did not by itself lead to new experiments in church life or worship, while the new creeds sprang from that new experience out of which arose the new ways of being a community and of worship. They began therefore to function in the communities which had come to life along with them.

We want to deal particularly with these new creeds. They are typical and representative enough for our time. The new way of confessing the faith as it is growing in the young churches of the third world is such a vast problem that it demands special attention.

## THE NEW WAY OF CONFESSING THE FAITH

People look first of all for new creeds which briefly and firmly set out what has again become certainty and what they will stand for in the world. Often the new creeds say first *why* one believes. This generation feels the need to say why and at which point one has again found the connection with the biblical tradition of the centuries. Then follows *what* one believes as a matter of accountability first of all to oneself, and then also to the others. This faith is recognized by others in the believing community which one has voluntarily joined. So this way of confessing becomes a unifying bond. Usually the element of praise, thanksgiving, turning from oneself towards God also enters into it by way of liturgy and hymns. This faith then begins to operate as the norm for preaching, celebrating and one's attitude towards life. It is transmitted as witness in both its prophetic and missionary aspects. It is passed on to the younger generation as the best thing one has found in one's own life. And it lays the foundation for a life of service, *diakonia,* to the world.

These creeds are usually short. Occasionally one or other will develop into wider reflection, which then will lead to a new creed.

The reason why one's faith is no longer seen in the old credal formulae as of practical value in life does not lie in the fact that isolated sentences in them no longer mean much to us, such as the virgin birth, the descent into hell, the resurrection of the body, and others, as was the case in the controversy about the Apostles' Creed in Germany round about 1890, but also before and after that date. The real malaise is that we cannot meaningfully experience what is specific to our age, the 'absolute Kulturschwelle' (cultural bar), the self-transcendence towards man and the world of the post-industrial cybernetic era, within the narrow space of the words of that creed. Our world is still constantly expanding in wave upon wave of a new self-realization within this world, and this brings consequences with it which affect our life right down to its roots. Our life is changing through increasing power, automation, aeronautics, eugenics, planetization, ABC-weapons, and the task to bring the world to fulfillment in universal brotherhood. All this creates a new personal awareness of privilege, glory and responsibility, but also of anxiety for the 'neighbour', and, after Auschwitz and Hiroshima, also for what this neighbour can do to us. It remains an ambivalent situation of grandeur and misery, of success and failure. At the same time we see the future as a historical mission, 'a laboratory of possibilities'. The Apostles' Creed no doubt points to the history of salvation and implies an eschatology but the living experience of the centuries which it represents has no room for the dramatic experience we are going through and the proclamation of re-gained certainties. This is why we need new creeds formulated in a way which can cope with this. And so there has been an explosion of new professions of faith and creeds within the framework of services for young people and alternative communities:[2] exclamations, acclamations, biblical summaries or paraphrases, adaptations of the Apostles' Creed or brand-new creations. Some look more like a manifesto or action programme than a creed. Sometimes they are naïve, crude, a mixture of old and new styles or different uses of language. But they are always genuine, real, and 'close to man'.[3] Occasionally they have been drafted by individuals such as H. Gollwitzer, H. Oosterhuis, D. Sölle or S. Zink.[4] They may also have originated in a community of believers. Some are already a little dated, like some of the professions of faith produced by Liberal Protestants, Mennonites or Remonstrants. Others are very recent, like the creeds of the United Church of Canada or the United Church of Christ in the USA.[5] Occasionally there appears to be no objection to a creed composed by an individual, who is apparently blessed with the gift of sensing exactly what all are feeling. This has happened more than once in church history as is shown by the *Confessio Belgica* and the *Confessio Augustana*. Among the new usable credal formulae there are some which so happily combine the original intent of the revelation with the voice of tradition that, as new attempts, they are not falling far behind the classical peace and beauty of the old creeds.

### THE CONTENTS

Like flowing lava, the texts show how hard the struggle was to express our own new experience of life in words taken from the credal tradition. In general one may say that the original biblical intent, as understood in the light of the present state of hermeneutics, has been genuinely interpreted. The original biblical message has been brought out again, and the biblical language has been preserved. It is necessary to be re-initiated into the biblical 'abc' of the original words and concepts of the Old and New Testaments to be able to accept this new way of confessing one's belief. This is why usually the triadic structure of the creed and sometimes that of the economy of salvation and the Trinity have been preserved simply because this new way of confessing imposes it.

It is curious to see how biblical-messianic the slant is in the new creeds. The point is not the general trend towards religion or the appeal of the eastern religions although our age is full of neo-gnostic, theosophical, anthroposophical, astrological and other movements. The question is far more about right and justice, world-socialism and world-peace. The meaning, purpose and destiny of man and his world belong to God's kingdom, which He is building up, pushes towards, and in which He wants to involve man's co-operation. This plan also embraces our own little lives. Historically we are conditioned to pursue this great Future. God pursues this plan against all opposition. The young people who live in modern world metropolises and confess their faith have no illusion whatever about the realities of this world. They are aware of the idols, and not blind to the 'demons'. They are aware of guilt, even of the guilt which is wiped off. They frankly accept their own weakness and failures. Jesus, the Messiah, is not simply the example, the paradigm of life as individual or in community. He also is Saviour, Redeemer, Lord. He brought to light God's loving intent about man and the world. His life reflected, and thus proclaimed, this intent. In his eschatological and normative human existence one can see what was meant by man and his situation in the world. According to the view of our corrupt world he went too far in trying to put the truth into practice. This is why he was done away with. But he has not been put away. God did him justice, showed that he was right and raised him to the status of Son of Man who, from then on, pursues his purpose and his life in and for the Kingdom. In the Spirit he appeals to men who, in a minor or major way, individually and communally, wish to live in, and serve this kingdom. Thus the main trend of contemporary belief is expressed in numerous varieties and accents.

A few Evangelical *Landeskirchen* have accepted these new creeds, with an eye, among other things, on these dynamic groups and forms of worship. This is possible because something of the multi-functional purpose of the old way of confessing is carried on in the new.

Here, too, with other assumptions and in a wholly different context, people are asked whether they wish to believe and accept the consequences of their choice. Here, too, it is briefly and summarily explained what it is ultimately about. People from numerous denominations find here some mutual recognition and discover here the bond of a new community with its own obligations. Hymns of thanks and praise obviously find expression in this way of confessing the faith. Thus these new creeds constitute a new rule for faith, preaching, celebrating and a new attitude to life. As a witness, the missionary and prophetic content is passed on to the outside, while it is the 'treasury of the heart' to which the young are initiated. It evokes in the believer a preparedness, commitment and spirit of service over against the sin of inertia, laziness and indifference.

OLD AND NEW

Thus the new creeds and professions of faith serve along with the old creeds which are not replaced by them, at least not for the present, and perhaps never will be. We have no other documents of the faith of the centuries nor of ecumenical Christendom which are so authoritative. This is why the old creeds will continue to be used, e.g., at baptism or at the eucharist. Because of that the others will prove how badly they are needed, whether in an educational establishment, at the house-mass, or in training. As 'brief formulae' they are wanted in catechetics and religious education because they can be adapted to every age and phase of life.[6] Perhaps one day every believer will be able to express, for himself and for others, in a flashlike way what to him or her appears as imperishable and what cannot be surrendered in the faith of the Scriptures. The new creeds are not produced along with the old ones simply to take us back to these old ones. They are there, side by side with the old ones, as re-interpretations which express what we mean when our own generation recites again the old formula.

There are people who think that the need for renewal has been satisfied with some slight revision of the Apostles' Creed, either by abbreviating it or slightly expanding it. They think that enough has been done about a re-edition of the Creed by slightly adjusting it to our age. In our view all these attempts at some slight adjustment of the Creed have failed because this does not answer the need to find there the expression of what is necessary for the needs of our own time. A paraphrase of the Creed, as provided by Jörg Zink, is already no longer a straightforward objective creed, but rather an explanation of it.[7]

That the Apostles' Creed does not explicate our need for the expression of our faith today is also proved by the extensive re-interpreting commentaries required by the modern explanations of it, and people

today rightly pursue this task, as has been done by people like Pannen-
berg and Ratzinger. The very fact that in practice re-formulations are
necessary to make the Creed meaningful to people shows that, without
this, it is difficult to live by it.

The updating of the old Creed by touching it up with a revision of the
text is useless. One cannot break up the cathedral of Chartres and put
the isolated parts together again to set it up in a wider space. It would
break down the architectural norm which made it.

The new way of confessing the faith should be allowed to grow side
by side with the old one out of a new creative impulse; it should be
renewed both in form and content as the contemporary reinterpretation which is never quite 'ready' but requires constant rectifi-
cation. This is because we live in an age of continuous reflexion which
never feels satisfied but renews itself incessantly.

In the meantime we have to keep on listening to the old symbols,
even if they sound alien to us, because original insights and truths may
acquire new importance in new contexts which shows that under the
emotional pressures of our age we may have neglected precisely those
insights. When all is said and done, these old documents represent the
voice of the dead (Chesterton). It is also necessary to maintain the
harmony between ourselves and the Catholicism of a particular age and
the way in which other centuries understood the faith.


PROFESSING THE FAITH ECUMENICALLY

The ecumenical professing of the faith will find more encouragement
in the new ways of expressing Christian belief than in the old formulae
because the latter were meant to be different from each other. We are
all constantly facing the same problems of the world and how we
should live in it, and we are learning to approach this problem in a
homogeneous and universal way.

But such an ecumenical expression of belief can no longer be expressed in a single doctrinal text in the way the Apostles' Creed acquired a monopoly in the West, at least. It will be pluralistic, first of all
because of regional, racial, cultural and religious differences. Then
there is the matter of the situation in which we find ourselves. It makes
a lot of difference whether one is a believer facing the classic religions
in India, or under a Communist regime, or in the continent of the
theology of liberation, or in the welfare states of the West. All this
makes the question of mutual acceptance imperative: can we mutually
accept each other's faith in the context of world-wide denominational
differences and can we test each other's creeds on this basis? [8]

Thus the new kinds of creed, like those mentioned as functioning in

Canada and the USA, will be first accepted in the national Churches and in the denominational groups one belongs to throughout the world. Starting from there they may achieve acceptance when other denominational groups throughout the world can recognize themselves in this formulation of the creed and see such a creed as the voice of the universal Church. Thus agreement on essentials might create greater coherence in a pluralistic application and expression of it. Only when these creeds are mutually accepted in the World Church—whether through use in practice or through official recognition by the Council— they could acquire the same canonical and universal force as authoritative and normative, which the old credal formulae have had up till now. Whether this will succeed, which would be the new creeds and how many would concur in such a unitary formula it is too early to assert. What is certain is that all such formulae must grow out of the Churches' communal practice of the faith and that they will need the maturity and the polish of the centuries. The need for and the pondering on such a polyphonous collective expression of the faith will go on. It looks as if the climax of this creative impetus has already been passed, like the students' protest and the counter-cultural movement. But appearance is deceptive. The passionate desire continues to smoulder under the surface. One sees this in the fact that almost every theologian of some calibre who thinks he understands something about the faith for the present and the future tries to express this in a creed which is sufficiently contemporary to allow many to join him in his way of formulating it. The level already achieved is shown by the attempts made by Küng, Rahner, Schoonenberg and P. Smulders.[9] Schillebeeckx, too, can be counted with them.[10] Schoonenberg's formula shows, with all its novelty, such a balance of old and new, of scriptural intent and the centuries-old tradition, that it may give us a taste of what we may expect of the way in which such a rejuvenating formula may come about. This is why I print it at the end of this article.[11]

I believe in God whom we may call 'Abba, Father' in the Spirit of Jesus, the Creator of the beginning and of the future.
And in Jesus, God's Servant and beloved Son.
Who wholly came from God to us and in whom God wished to live with all his plenitude.
Who laboured to heal us, broke through human limitations and spoke words of eternal life.
Who therefore was rejected but suffered to liberate us and died on the cross.
Who is raised by God to live in us and to 'stand' in the future of all creation.

I believe in the Spirit of God and of Jesus, who speaks to us through the prophets and leads us into the whole truth.
I profess God's kingdom now and for all eternity, and in the Church which may expect and serve this kingdom.
I profess the liberation from sin and power to love.
And the new creation where justice prevails and God will be all in all.

## Notes

1. Karl Rahner, *Schriften zur Theologie,* VIII, pp. 153–64; IX, pp. 242–56. Cf. Alex Stock, *Kurzformeln des Glaubens. Zur Unterscheidung des christlichen bei Karl Rahner* (Einsiedeln, Zürich, Cologne, 1971).

2. Texts can be found in vol. II of Roman Bleistein, *Kurzformel des Glaubens* (2 vols.); Gerhard Ruhbach, ed., *Glaubensbekenntnisse für unsere Zeit* (Gütersloh, 1971); Heinz G. Schmidt (ed.), *Zum Gottesdienst Morgen* (Wuppertal, 1969); Eimert Pruim, *Oude en nieuwe woorden voor God, wereld en kerk* (coll. texts) (Delft, n.d.); Gerhard Ruhback a.o. (ed.), *Bekenntnis in Bewegung. Ein Informations—und Diskussionsbuch* (Göttingen, 1969).

3. Of the many articles on this subject we mention: W. Beinert, 'Die alten Glaubensbekenntnisse und die neue Kurzformeln' in *Communio* 1 (1972), pp. 97–114; id., 'Kurzformeln des Glaubens—Reduktion oder Konzentration?' in *Theologisch-praktische Quartalschrift* 122 (1974), pp. 105–17; Karl Lehmann, 'Bedarf das Glaubensbekenntnis einer Neufassung?' in *Veraltetes Glaubensbekenntnis?* (Regensburg 1968), pp. 125–86) id., 'Die Grundbotschaft des neuen Testaments. Kurzformeln des christlichen Glaubens', in *Handbuch der Verkündigung,* vol. I (1970), pp. 274–95; id., in *Gegenwart des Glaubens* (Mainz, 1974), pp. 175–99; Albrecht Peters, 'Moderne evangelische Glaubensbekenntnisse und katholische Kurzformeln des Glaubens', in *Kerygma und Dogma* 19 (1973), pp. 232–53; Jozef Ratzinger, 'Nocheinmal: Kurzformeln des Glaubens', in *Internationale Kath. Zeitschrift* (1973), pp. 258–64.

4. Bleistein, vol. II, pp. 19, 72, 113, 118.

5. Bleistein, vol. II, pp. 25 and 33.

6. Bleistein, *Kurzformeln des Glaubens,* vol. I: *Prinzip einer modernen Religionspädagogik.*

7. Bleistein, vol. II, pp. 113–17.

8. Lukas Vischer, *Veränderung der Welt—Bekehrung der Kirchen* (Frankfurt a.M., 1976), pp. 13–38.

9. Bleistein, vol. II, pp. 67, 86–93, 102, 'Credo's onderweg', p. 28.

10. E. Schillebeeckx, *Gerechtigheid en liefde, genade en bevrijding* (Bilthoven, 1977), pp. 782–83.

11. Bleistein, vol. II, p. 67; P. Schoonenberg, *Ein Gott der Menschen* (Einsiedeln, 1964), p. 204.

Rene Marle

# Giving an Account of the Hope
# That Is in Us

INTRODUCTION: TWO MAJOR DOCUMENTS

AMONG the many 'confessions of faith' published recently two merit
particular attention: the document 'Faith and Order' of the Ecumenical
Council of Churches, propounded at the conference held at Accra
(Ghana) in 1974; and the document produced by the Synod of the
dioceses of the Federal Republic of Germany in 1975.[1] Leaving aside
the question of the privileged nature of their provenance, we must
nevertheless grant the special interest and importance of documents
produced either by a large ecumenical community or by a whole
Church.

### UNDERSTANDABLE DIFFERENCES

Their different origins lead us to expect that the two documents will
not be identical on all points. First there is a difference in general tone.

The German synodal text was intended to be a finished, and for the
time being at least, definitive statement. It thus appears as a unified,
firmly constructed whole. Although it expresses views of formulae
propounded by different members of the Synod, it bears the mark of a
single author, the theologian J. B. Metz, and there was no secret made
of this.

At least in its first part, the text on Faith and Order also bears the
mark of a single writer, Moltmann, who was an important figure at

Accra, and whose style and ideas are easily recognizable in the first, strictly theological, part of the document. This first part is also an impressive, unified whole. But the Commission on Faith and Order wanted to publish it to the Churches accompanied by a series of other documents. After the fundamental document, a series of texts discuss 'problems of Christian hope' in certain 'challenges' (the challenge of African Christianity, the challenge of the oppressed, the challenge of development and change, the challenge of disillusionments, the challenge of urban everyday life . . . ) before the concluding text reminds us of the 'unity of witness' towards which all Christians should aspire. Finally in the form of appendices, a certain number of 'affirmations of hope' are proposed, in various forms (liturgical, catechetical, personal) to 'help the Churches realize their hope'.

The document on Faith and Order is intended as an open proposal. It reflects the ecumenical community which created it, and this community is still in the course of being formed, 'in labour', we could say, and not as yet united. The relatively composite nature of the text is intentional: 'This report by the very diversity of its form and content invites Christians throughout the world, to broach the fundamental question', the question to which each Christian has begun to work an answer for himself.

However even in this, it is not so very different from the German Synod's document, which speaks of the 'many bearers of our hope' and wants its witness to be an 'invitation to hope'.

Of course, it is possible to note a certain number of minor differences in the content of the two documents.

The doctrinal content of the German Synod's text is somewhat more developed than that of the Constitution's. It contains certain elements which one would not expect to find in the WCC document (for example, an allusion to the sacrament of penance), or which the latter would have no reason to include (for example, the intention expressed to make 'a new relationship to the history and faith of the Jewish people').

Perhaps I should also point out in the German Synod's document a more formally expressed concern with 'Catholic' orthodoxy, with the reference from the start to 'the whole fulness of the Church's credo, which also forms the basis of this confessional text'. But as we shall see, this credo is, for practical purposes, also the basis of the document on Faith and Order.

Without over-emphasizing the difference, we may also note the more immediately Christological approach of the document on Faith and Order: 'Affirmation of the hope that is in Christ' is the title of the basic text. And at the beginning there is the statement: 'The first foundation of this hope is the revelation of the trinitarian God in and through Jesus

Christ'. Whereas the German Synod's document begins with the 'God of our hope' whose name is 'graven deep in the history of the hope and sufferings of mankind'; this God who is also 'the God of Abraham, Isaac and Jacob', who 'created heaven and earth' and whom 'we publicly confess as well as the Jewish people and the people of Islam'. However, a bit further on the same text clearly expresses 'our hope in Jesus Christ'.

## REMARKABLE SIMILARITIES

However, the similarities between the two documents are much more striking than the differences. When it formulated its confession founded on hope, the German Synod was aware of its 'bond with the Ecumenical Council of Churches which has summoned all Christians to give an account of their hope'.

The two texts are similar both in their motivations and their construction. In the 1971 world conference at Louvain which preceded the Accra conference, Dr Lukas Vischer, the Secretary for Faith and Constitution, declared that the time had come to go beyond the scrutiny of the many problems involved in the question of unity, and listen to the call from the world of unbelievers, to try to 'formulate together the fundamental data of faith'. He then invited the assembled Churches and Christians to examine, in the words of the First Letter to Peter: 'How shall we give an account together, today of the hope that is in us?' The German Synod also wanted to come down to essentials because of the radical nature of the question confronting believers in our time: 'We must be careful not to allow the many questions of detail make us neglect the questions that have arisen among us in society: questions about the very meaning of being a Christian in our time'.

There are also similarities in the way in which these texts were constructed: they were not the result of a single person's or group's inspiration, but proceeded from patient working together, even though, as we said earlier, their definitive versions bore the marks of certain particular authors. The witness that Faith and Order wished to bear to the common faith and hope of Christians was to be the fruit of a *pia conspiratio,* in Calvin's fine phrase. The Accra conference made its attempt at a formulation after attempts that had been made on every continent by the most varied groups. The Accra formulation was designed then to go back out to all these Churches and Christian communities. Likewise the German Synod's text was the result of considerable comings and goings between editors, the commission, the assembly.

The common basic orientation of the two texts is also clear. Both documents are not trying to give an account of static truths but of a transforming dynamism leading to action. In both documents hope is presented as the direct objection of confession. The Faith and Order text speaks of the 'power of this hope' which is 'the work of the Holy Spirit in us', whereas the German Synod's text sees a 'renewal of hope' to be expressed in a 'manifestation of Spirit and power for our time'.

But hope cannot stand by itself. It is founded on faith. 'The first foundation of this hope', declares the Faith and Order text, 'is the revelation of the Trinitarian God in and through Jesus Christ', and the German Synod proposes to 'speak publicly of our hope which is founded on faith'. This hope has 'a content and a foundation', which it is trying to give an account of in order to see what practical commitments it involves.

This foundation and this content of Christian hope are essentially identical in both documents: Faith in the Trinity and in Christ. The Trinitarian structure of the Christian faith, the foundation of its hope, is brought out very clearly in the Faith and Order text which begins with the revelation in and through Jesus Christ, goes on to the working of the power of the Spirit, to the fulfilment of hope 'in the hands of the Father of Jesus Christ'. The German Synod text begins with the 'God of our hope' who 'made himself known as Father' through his 'eternal Word' which 'became man, one of us'. Later, it goes on to speak of the Holy Spirit as the 'living foundation' of the Church's unity, who as the 'Holy Spirit of the glorified Lord' is the 'inner strength of the confidence' of this Church.

Although the order in which the fundamental affirmations of traditional faith are made is different, in both documents this faith is presented as unfolding from the starting point of the mystery of Christ who died and rose from the dead. The revelation of the Trinitarian God in and through Jesus Christ occurs first through his messianic mission, the meaning of which is recalled by the text on Faith and Order: 'When the blind receive their sight, and the lame walk, lepers are cleansed and the deaf hear, and the dead are raised up, and the poor have good news preached to them, then God's time has come' (Mt. 11:5). Christian faith echoes this Gospel and its business is to proclaim it. The German Synod mentions the attraction that the figure of Jesus has for today because he continues to arouse consciences, widen horizons and mobilize generosity. But it also stresses that his message and his example would lose their real meaning and all their force if they were not rooted in the person who is the eternal Son of the Father. Furthermore it adds:'This history of the hope of our faith has acquired an invincible nature in the resurrection of Jesus'. For Christian faith, Jesus is not merely a simple model, however fine, from the past. He is living, and still today he makes all prison walls fall down and all tombs open. To express, as the Synod puts it, this central affirmation of the 'credo of primitive Christianity' (referring to 1 Cor. 15: 3–5) both documents find plenty of support in references and formulae from Scripture. But the important point in both cases is the central place given to the resurrection.

Christ's resurrection is the guarantee of the resurrection of the dead and the promise of eternal life. On this point both texts are equally clear and eloquent. 'By his sacrifice and his resurrection', declares the Faith and Order text, 'we are filled with an invincible hope in eternal life, in spite of sin, death and the powers of evil'. And further on: 'We also expect the resurrection of the dead, and we know that our hope will never be fulfilled in this world for as long as the dead remain dead. This hope makes us capable of sacrifice in the name of love; it gives us hope for the dead, and consolation about our own death. This is also why we yearn for eternal life in which we will share God's glory in its fulness'. The German Synod text is no less explicit: 'Looking at Jesus, crucified and risen from the dead, we also hope for the resurrection of the dead'. This hope counters a more and more widespread attitude that tends to hide death, make mourning shamefaced, and obliterate the memory of the dead. 'In this situation we confess our hope in the resurrection of the dead. This is not just a utopia; it is rooted in the evidence of the resurrection of Christ'. This gives us the assurance that the dead, even those who are now forgotten remain 'unforgettably in the mind of the living God and live forever in him'.

Faith which is the foundation of hope is lived out day by day in the Church, to which both documents give an important place and assign a fundamentally identical function. This is summed up in a few words in the Faith and Order text: 'Thanks to the gifts of the Holy Spirit, we are freed to live a life of reconciliation, to live in a new community and serve our society'. But the text also develops the meaning of this mission: 'The Church, in the name of the knowledge given to it of the Word of God, raises a prophetic voice to speak for a more human society. It intercedes incessantly for the world. Above all it should appear as the sign of a new community among people, which is the communion of the one holy, universal and apostolic Church. A community which listens and gives thanks; a community in which we can freely seek the truth without risk; a community of reconciled people; a community of service which is freely and totally at the service of one another and of all people, particularly those who are rejected by society; a community following in the steps of Jesus which freely accepts the poverty imposed on it and tries to make good use of the wealth it is given; a community of spontaneous celebrations in a world planned down to the last detail'. The German Synod also sets the Church 'in Jesus' footsteps'. 'Following in his footsteps is the price we pay for our bond with him, the price of our orthodoxy; this is the only road to the renewal of the Church'. This Church is itself the first beginnings of the 'new creation'. 'Our Church is a community of hope'. A community which is open and which communicates the truths by which it lives: 'More than ever we owe ourselves and our world the witness of a community of hope, which contains within it many living forms of being together in his name, and which continually creates and promotes others'.

Faith which bears the dynamism of hope and to which both documents witness, is faith realized in practice.

Faith in the resurrection of Christ does not allow us simply a happy rest. The German Synod stresses the link between the cross and the resurrection. Our hope must live through a life of suffering and death. When we look hopefully at the cross, we cannot forget 'the unknown history of the world's sufferings'. 'Only if we Christians pay attention to the dark prophecies of suffering' formulated by Jesus in Matthew 25, 'and if we are ready to help, do we hear and confess the message full of hope in Jesus' own sufferings'. And the Faith and Order text reminds us that our hope in the resurrection must not distract us from the work to be done now. 'Longing for God does not mean abandoning the world to death. It leads us to an ardent struggle for God's rights over his creation. Brothers, because of your hope in a new heaven and a new earth, be faithful to this earth!' 'The love of Christ makes us able to work to transform this world into a more human world, and it obliges us to do so'.

Thus both texts do not hesitate to include in their profession of faith the justified affirmation of Christian hope the mention of certain disorders and wrongs in the world in which this faith and this hope must bear witness. Although it points out clearly the limits of all social hope, the Faith and Order text holds that 'actual social utopias can come into line with the eschatalogical reality of the Kingdom of God'. And there is a 'hope common to all mankind' for whose fulfilment believers must strive. The German Synod, speaking for and to a more limited community, can be more precise in its enumeration of the struggles which Christian faith and hope must engage in against the disorders and wrongs of the world: the huge inequality in the division of wealth, even between Churches, the threats to the weak and innocent, and even to human life as such, the many forms of oppression and manipulation.

Both documents use a significant word: challenge. This word is used by both to express their concern with what needs to be done today.

And of course the situation we all are in today has nothing to do with differences in Christian belief. Both documents ask radical questions, thus seeking what is fundamental to and constitutive of Christian belief. All confess the same foundation Word. Both documents, whatever their differences in form and detail, show impressive agreement in their perception of this Word and its resonances.

*Translated by Dinah Livingstone*

*Notes*

1. The Faith and Order document 'Giving an account of the hope that is in us', with all its various elements has been published in English by the WCC in the volume *Uniting in Hope* (Geneva, 1975), pp. 25–80. There is a cyclostyled text of the same collection in French. The fundamental part of the document: 'Affirmation of the hope that is in Christ' was published in *Istina* XX (1975), pp. 191–94. The German Synod's document is 'Unsere Hoffnung. Ein Bekenntnis zum Glauben in dieser Zeit', in *Gemeinsame Synode der Bistümer in der Bundesrepublik Deutschland.* (Freiburg, Basle, Vienna, 1976), pp. 84–111.

# PART VI

*Attempt at a Synthesis*

Lukas Vischer

# An Ecumenical Creed? An Attempt at a Synthesis

UNITY IN FAITH—DIVISIONS BETWEEN THE CHURCHES

HOW CAN the one faith be expressed? Can this be done in a creed? The authors writing in this volume are visibly cautious in their answers to this question. They talk in detail about the nature and possible functions of creeds. They mention points which would have to be covered in an ecumenical creed. But they leave open the question whether the Churches could come together in acknowledgement of a common creed. An ecumenical creed? The question mark after the title is certainly not removed by the arguments in this volume; if anything it is underlined. Is a creed a proper way of bringing about unity in faith?

The Churches continue to face each other as divided 'denominations'. The term 'creed' is connected primarily, not with community of belief, but with the particularity of the individual Churches. Many disputed questions have been resolved, and there has been some coming together, but the Churches still remain divided from each other and it is hard to envisage that an ecumenical creed alone could hold them together. Quite apart from the fact that they have still not reached agreement on many points of doctrine, they also differ from one another in the value they place on the necessity and the function of formulated creeds. While in one Church creeds have a fundamental importance, in the others they have only a subordinate rôle. Not all denominations are also 'confessions' in the strict sense, and it is therefore not just a simple matter of finding the one creed which will meet the needs of the whole ecumenical community. Before a creed can acquire unifying force, there must be agreement about the place of a creed in the life of the Church. This difficulty appears clearly in the six 'denominational' articles in this volume. The authors automatically start from different ideas about a creed. The difference is revealed particularly clearly when two Churches embark on serious discussions. They then discover that they attach different degrees of significance to the conclusions they have been able to formulate in accordance with their different understandings of a creed, and are therefore unable to adopt them in the same way.

The diversity which is a feature of Christendom today goes far beyond the diversity of 'denominational' traditions. The differences which divide the denominations from one another are the product of a relatively limited history. Almost all of them originated in particular stages of European and, later, American history. While the denominations differ from one another, they nevertheless belong to the same world. They are linked by a common, and constantly recalled, history. In this respect the missionary movement of recent centuries has created a new situation. By taking seriously the command to preach the Gospel to the ends of the earth, the Churches took the 'confessions' into new areas and at the same time transcended the limited '*Oikuménè* of the denominations'. New worlds with new questions appeared on the Church's horizon. It may have been possible to suppress these questions for a long time, but they are now demanding attention with irresistible force. What does it mean to preach the Gospel in the sphere of Asiatic religions? (Chun) What form must the creed assume in the context of African religions? The disputes of previous centuries will not necessarily be irrelevant to answering such questions; they could in many ways provide models. However, the new issues must also be recognised as autonomous. The *Oikuménè* has been enlarged and enriched by new voices not envisaged in the 'denominational' traditions. As one example among many, take phenomena such as the independent African Churches, at first sight at least, so strange. They cannot be fitted into the familiar traditions, and if they are an injustice is being done them. They are rather proof that the *Oikuménè* today includes new worlds. If they were adequately to reflect this new situation, the six 'denominational' articles in this volume would perhaps have had to be supplemented by a series of these new and unusual voices.

It would nevertheless be inadequate to contrast the limited '*Oikuménè* of the denominations' with the *Oikuménè* enlarged by the missionary expansion. This is not the entire explanation of the diversity which characterizes Christendom today. That stems much more from the fact that the Churches in all parts of the world are facing new issues. The *Oikuménè* of the denominations has not only been placed in a wider context; it has also in itself been profoundly shaken. The existing answers are no longer adequate. The Churches find themselves thrown into new and previously unexplored conflicts. The result is a diversity of answers which often do not coincide with denominational traditions. They are leading to new schools, movements, communities and groups. They do not obliterate denominational boundaries, but they reduce their importance. A strange new community has come into being, a community of questioning and searching, a community of fundamental agreement and, in many respects, also of fundamental uncertainty, a community of new conflicts which have not yet been resolved.

A creed worthy of the name ecumenical would have to do justice to this vast diversity. It would have to sum up the faith in such a way that all sides could recognize themselves in it. Is it conceivable that a creed should be capable of this? In view of the present diversity doubts are more than justified. And yet the unity in faith must be given expression. In spite of all doubts about the possibility of an ecumenical creed, all the contributors to this volume seem to be in agreement about this. So how is it to come about? Are we to treat the new community which has already come into being as unity and try to give it a common articulation in a contemporary and constantly renewed profession of faith? Or should we accept that by means of the World Council of Churches the Churches 'give particular form to hope in the given context and thereby proclaim the universality of their faith' (Højen)? Or do we need a new sort of creed? Certainly hypothetical discussions about the nature and possible functions of a creed are not enough. The question is rather what specific steps are required to bring us closer to that 'visible unity in one faith and one eucharistic community'.

## TWO PATHS

How could we arrive at a creed with ecumenical validity? Two paths suggest themselves. The common basis could be found either in the creeds of the early Church or in a new creed still to be drawn up. It is worth while examining these two paths in more detail.

### A Common Basis in the Creeds of the Early Church

A return to the creeds of the early Church is not to be rejected out of hand. Are they not part of a tradition on which all the Churches draw in one way or another, and could they not therefore provide what Heron calls 'an enduring point of reference'? True, just as the Churches set a different value on the importance of creeds in general, they also have different views about the importance of the creeds of the early Church. Some see in the 'ancient and venerable creeds of the undivided Church' the starting point for the theological study required by modern problems; even though they do not 'say everything that belongs to the faith', the necessary propositions can be derived from them (Damaskinos). Others are much more cautious in their assessment. They are much more keenly aware of the enormous gulf between the thought which is expressed in the ancient creeds and the presuppositions which govern modern theological thinking. The different evaluations of the creeds of the early Church today exist not only between different Churches, but, interestingly, more and more within one and the same Church (Tomkins). All the Churches are, however, agreed that the creeds of the early Church have a special place in the tradition of the Church. They recall those first centuries in which decisions were taken with far-reaching implications for the teaching and structure of the Church. No Church can come unscathed out of a confrontation with that formative period. The creeds must also be taken seriously as testimonies because they were taken seriously by all the generations which preceded us, which means that a community through the ages is inconceivable without respect for the creeds.

Three points are of enormous importance:

(i) It is plain that the creeds of the early Church belong to a particular time and place in history. The process of the formation of both the Apostles' Creed and the Niceno-Constantinopolitan Creed can be described in detail (Heron, Kannengiesser). There is probably general agreement that this admission also has theological importance. The ancient creeds are not timeless summaries of the faith. They are witnesses from a certain period, and if they retain validity for later periods they retain it as witnesses from that particular period. The Apostles' Creed was perhaps envisaged from the beginning as a summary of the faith to a greater extent than the Niceno-Constantinopolitan. Its origin is in the liturgy and catechesis, and it therefore presents us with the doctrinal tradition of a particular period. The Niceno-Constantinopolitan, on the other hand, is a witness to a decision which the Church had to make in the face of a particular threat to apostolic truth. It was originally not a general statement won, in Moltmann's words, 'at the cost of abstraction', but a confession of actual belief.

Both creeds have changed in character in the course of history. They have been adopted by the Church in a way that has allowed their original place in history to fade into the background. This change is not generally taken sufficiently into account, although it is obvious that a creed changes its function when it is no longer a Council's decision against a heresy, but is recited in the liturgy Sunday by Sunday, and still more when it is taken into the Church's constitution or some other legal text. The ancient creeds owe their prominence not solely to their propositional content, but also to the 'integrative role' (Modras) they have acquired in their adoption by the Church. However, this double level in the significance and action of the creeds leads inevitably to a tension. If the creeds are to be taken seriously as witnesses to their period, their meaning can only be elucidated by a process of interpretation, not through mere repetition and recitation. But does not this go rather a long way towards casting doubt on their integrative role? The conclusion is inescapable. The creeds should not be taken primarily as timeless 'unchangeable formulas', which guarantee 'continuity' (Moltmann), but as essential fixed elements in a constantly developing process of interpretation and updating.

(ii) It is also plain that the creeds 'do not say all that belongs to the faith'. Many issues which had already arisen when the creeds were composed are not dealt with. The Apostles' Creed selects a particular group of kerygmatic statements, and the Niceno-Constantinopolitan reflects a particularly crucial dispute. The two creeds therefore, a fortiori, do not give answers to many questions which are current today. When we are challenged to give an account of the hope that is in us, we cannot, or can only in rare cases, fall back directly on the creeds. This fact becomes particularly clear in catechesis. Here the creeds are of only limited importance. Catechesis has to give a summary account of all the Church's teaching, and, while at appropriate places it will attempt to explain the meaning of the creeds and interpret their content, it will not be able to keep exclusively to the creeds. It will emphasize certain statements in the creeds and let others slip into the background. Above all, it will bring up topics which can be derived only indirectly, or not at all, from the creeds. The tradition on which the Church draws is wider than the creeds. In order to be able to give genuine and relevant account, the Church must therefore be in a position to fall back on this tradition.

(iii) Is it possible to bring out the permanent validity of the ancient creeds by means of abridgments, paraphrases or interpolations? Attempts in this direction are certainly legitimate. Abridged formulations can make clear what elements of the ancient creeds are really indispensable to contemporary needs and which might, under certain circumstances, be neglected without abridging the tradition. Paraphrases can make us realize how the same statements would have to read in modern language: they can open up the text. Interpolations can interpret and apply the creed with reference to a particular question, a procedure already employed by the Council of Nicaea when it enriched an existing creed by adding polemical statements. They can also deal with topics which are not contained in the creeds but nevertheless must be mentioned. All these efforts circle essentially round the same question. They show that the creeds, to become intelligible, need interpretation and updating. In this respect they can perform important services. They can bridge the gap between the distant past and today. It is, however, exceedingly unlikely that any of these reformulations could ever replace the creeds of the early Church and become the common creed of the future. They draw their force from the full text and integrating power of the creeds. Therefore, if any attempt is made to draw on the creeds, it must use the genuine text and not a modified version. The creeds themselves will always remain more ecumenical than the reformulations suggested today (cf. H. van der Linde).

## A New Creed

The second possible path is that the common basis be found in a new creed. Is it conceivable that such a creed should be devised and formulated? Some of the contributors seem to envisage this as a possibility (Willis), while others rule it out in advance (Damaskinos). It must, however, be emphasized that the answer depends to a large extent on what is understood by a creed. Those who regard it as primarily an immediate response to a situation tend to accept the possibility. Those who see it as a binding and universally recognized statement on specific doctrines regard the attempt as both impossible and undesirable. All the contributors, however, agree that the Church must respond to new questions and agree further that the still divided Churches must speak as far as possible with one voice. Can the unity in the faith be given expression in this way?

Three considerations are of particular relevance in this context:

(i) Several contributors to this volume stress that a compelling occasion is required for the Church to express the common faith in binding form. The Councils of the early Church met because the truth and unity of the Church were threatened. They were not theological congresses, but assemblies which had proved necessary to meet a potential split. The point of this remark is obvious. A new creed cannot be planned. It cannot be drafted and composed by a commission on the basis of theoretical discussions. The compelling occasion is required. Only when they are faced by an inescapable challenge will those who have to speak find the courage to speak in binding terms. Only then will they speak with authority. Only then will they find a common language. Only then will the Church really listen to them. Correct though these observations are, they can be taken too far. They can be misused to evade the task the Church faces. Since no compelling occasion exists there is no need for a binding statement. But who can say with certainty that the occasion has not already come? Truth and unity are most profoundly endangered. A joint exposition of the Gospel could have a liberating effect on the whole Church and beyond. Of course, a new creed will be a gift of the Spirit. It cannot be programmed. But neither will it appear automatically one day without any preparation. That is why we need a constant common effort to express the meaning of the Gospel. Only when the possibility of a new creed is constantly before our eyes may it one day be granted to us. A stress on the need for a compelling occasion may be an expression of blindness and idleness.

(ii) However, a contemporary creed of this sort, if it were ever composed, could not perform the function which the creeds of the early Church performed for many centuries in the Church. It would make the meaning of the Gospel clear for today. It would give instruction and perhaps also lay down limits. But it would not be a bond of unity in the same sense as the old creeds. At the most it would be comparable with the Nicene Creed at the moment of its formulation. It would not acquire the unifying force which the creeds of the early Church later came to possess until it was adopted by the whole Church and specifically declared to be a bond of unity. We must beware of placing a possible new creed on the same level as the creeds of the early Church. A modern creed would probably lead at first to conflicts and disputes, and only after a considerable period would it appear whether the creed expressed the one faith in a form valid for the whole Church. A creed cannot be dreamt up to have immediate effect as a bond of unity! Indeed, we may ask whether it is desirable at all that new creeds should be adopted in the same way as the creeds of the early Church. Would not this be a way of unduly enlarging the common binding basis by adding a constant succession of new topics? Is it not better for the Church to give itself the greatest possible freedom of movement into the future? Is it not therefore advisable that contemporary creeds should remain contemporary creeds and not be burdened with additional functions? The more detailed and precise creeds have become, the greater has grown the distance which has separated the Churches from each other (Chun).

(iii) The call for a new creed inevitably brings up the question of the unity of the Church. Does not a contemporary creed need a common basis? Can the one faith be stated in a particular situation in a form valid for the whole Church, and can the statement really be heard by the whole Church, unless the Churches have already come together? In other words, unity, or at least a certain degree of unity, is the necessary precondition for a genuine contemporary confession of faith. The bond of unity must be at least strong enough for the Churches to recognize the 'compelling occasion' and respond in common. The boundaries of the denominations must be broken down sufficiently for the tradition of the Church to become a common inspiration. The World Council of Churches is a step in that direction. The common basis accepted by all the Churches makes possible a limited common witness, but it is not enough for a bond of unity. It leaves the diversity of 'confessions' essentially undisturbed. Agreement on the tradition, the source from which we draw, must therefore be extended and made deeper. Consensus is certainly not a confession of faith for our time, but a certain degree of consensus is nonetheless a necessary condition for confessing the faith in our time. As long as this degree is not reached, it is unlikely that a common new creed will come into existence.

## CONTEMPORARY CONFESSIONS OF FAITH IN THE CONTINUITY OF THE TRADITION

How can we go on from here? Both paths clearly lead to dilemmas. If we ask whether the common basis can be found in the creeds of the early Church, it appears that their validity can only be shown by the interpretation and updating of the tradition. If we ask whether a common basis can be found in a new creed, it appears that a new creed depends on a common understanding of the tradition. Can a solution be found among these contradictions? Can the contradictory conclusions be united in one view? The following considerations may make a contribution to this.

## 1. Respect for the Tradition

When the Church today talks about the Gospel, it speaks as the heir to a long tradition. Generations before it have sought to confess the same Gospel. It is essential that this tradition of confessing should be visibly present in the Church.

Certainly, every true confession of the Gospel is rooted in Jesus Christ, who 'confesses his own before his heavenly Father'. Only his confession makes the confession of the Church and its individual members possible at all (Moltmann). He intercedes for them and gives them the assurance that nothing can separate them from the love which was revealed in and through him. Every act of confession is therefore nothing other than a reference to his perfect confession. The Spirit has brought about such acts in all periods. He was at work in the apostles. He has constantly called new prophets and martyrs. He has acted in the Councils. He created a tradition of confessing, and where he is present today this whole tradition of confessing is always present too. It is essential that we call this to mind. In this process the early Church's confessions of faith have a special function.

It is not difficult to question the importance of the creeds of the early Church. In a period when their value was overestimated it may even have been important to question it. But today it is surely much more important to stress their limited importance. It is particularly important not to be led into false contrasts. The fact that the creeds are no guarantee of either truth or unity does not mean that they can contribute nothing to truth and unity. That their language is not contemporary does not mean that they have no contribution to make to contemporary statements. They are one of the signs which make the tradition of confessing present to us. They are only one of these signs. They cannot be isolated from the whole stream of the Church's life. They must be seen in association with scripture, with baptism and the eucharist, with the inherited practice of the Church, with the stories of confessors, etc. But within this diversity of signs they have an irreplaceable function. They remind us emphatically in their own way that the confession of Jesus Christ and the tradition of confessing created by him goes before us. 'The subjective credo has an objective credo of the Church as its inescapable point of reference, and this means a set of principles formulated in human words which includes at least the bible and the creeds of the early Church as basic documents of the faith', says Karl Barth in his study of Anselm of Canterbury (*Fides quaerens intellectum*, Zurich, 1931, p. 16). This is another reason for giving the creeds of the early Church a place in both liturgy and catechesis.

## 2. Confessing Ever Anew

But the other side is no less important. The Church must face the task of confessing anew. Christ, who confesses the Church before his heavenly Father, demands that the Church confess him today. He sends the Church out anew at every moment. No creed composed at one time says all that has to be said; none is complete. As the Church goes further on her way new questions arise which have to be answered. The task is therefore not to work now towards the definitive ecumenical creed. What is much more important is that the Churches should allow themselves to be drawn into a process of common ecumenical confessing. The confession required of them now will not be a final point. The rest of the future will bring new 'compelling occasions'. A fixed creed cannot guarantee the identity of the faith; truth can only be found in the struggle for the right interpretation' (Lang).

If the Churches really engage in this struggle, they will no longer be able to restrict themselves to developing their particular 'confessional' teachings and convictions. They will discover that the confessions of faith which constitute their particularity are no more than the testimony of a particular period, and that these alone are not an adequate source if they want to give a valid account of their faith. The 'confessions' can no longer serve as starting-points; they must be regarded rather as points of transition. Seeing them as an appropriate form of confessing the faith in a particular period will make them to some extent fluid. The broader and richer tradition which underlies all individual acts of confessing will then be able to break through afresh. Imbalances which in a particular period were not only justified, but even necessary, can be corrected. Dimensions which were neglected can be acknowledged once more. New impulses can be absorbed.

Various articles attempt to mention the topics which would have to be included today in an appropriate creed. Three of these receive particular prominence. A creed for today would have to speak in more detail than previous ones about the nature and mission of the Church (Dulles, Willis, Costas), about the creation and vocation of man (Damaskinos), and about ethical demands, especially those of social ethics (Højen, Costas). All three topics have an important part in the Church's experience; and all are today topics of extensive controversy. Joint statements could therefore be of immense importance for the preservation, not only of the Church's unity, but also of truth. And why should such statements not be produced? Why should the compelling occasion which gives the Church power to produce them not arise? The issue of the nature and mission of the Church, in particular, has been sufficiently clarified in recent decades for the leap to a joint statement to seem feasible.

Any attempt at a common statement will, however, have to face a serious difficulty. How can a creed intended as valid for the whole Church do justice to the immense diversity which is a feature of the Church today? A relevant confession must ultimately take place in particular situations. The risen Christ sends the disciples to particular human beings, all in their particular situations. Doesn't this mean that an ecumenical creed will be forced either to say nothing relevant or to do violence to the diversity of the situations? The dilemma can be solved if the occasion which compels the statement is felt in the same way in all situations. Such an occasion would exist, for example, if a danger which threatened the survival of the human race could be clearly defined. The dilemma can also be solved if the creed is recognized by the whole Church in a particular situation as exemplary. The Barmen Declaration could be cited as an example of such a procedure. However the dilemma can only be solved if there grows up in the Church a new awareness of and a new respect for the diversity of the situations. The common creed must not try to put itself in the place of the particular act of confessing in its situation; it must rather try to let itself be carried by this and try to stimulate it. The common creed will rather recall the sources on which confessing draws; it will use the language which is common to all and familiar to all. Particular acts of confessing will elaborate the creed and formulate it for particular audiences in language they can understand. The validity of the common utterance will not become fully clear until the diversity of particular voices in the Church becomes really audible.

The Faith and Order Commission's statement on the 'hope that is in us' (Accra 1974) is an attempt to link common and particular confessing (Marlé). It counterposes a common statement with a diversity of particular voices. The common statement calls to mind the unity which holds the Church together in the diversity of situations. The description of the diversity draws attention to the particularity of the individual situations. In this way both what includes in itself all the situations and the possible exemplary significance of particular creeds can be given due expression. Imperfect though the Faith and Order Commission's attempt may be in many respects, the form may nevertheless remain important for the future.

## 3. Common Structures

Finally, there is a further important aspect which must not be ignored. If this act of common ecumenical confession is to take place, the Church must be in a position to cope with it. Relevant creeds are not just a theological matter; they must in the end be accepted by the Church community. Theologians may think, draft and propose, but it is the Church which has final responsibility for the creed. For this reason it would be wrong to concentrate exclusively on the content of the creed; equally important is the question of the way in which relevant acts of confessing can take place. What structures are required to encourage common utterances? Who speaks for the Church? What processes can contribute to making the whole Church an effective party to the creed? If these questions are not asked, discussions on the way the Church confesses its faith will remain too 'Docetist'.

The Council of Nicaea will serve as an illustration. The common ecumenical confession was made possible because a new structure had been created. The instrument which became known as the 'ecumenical council' was an important precondition for relevant confessing in the fourth century. Without this structural innovation the Church would probably not have been able to deal with the new and important issues (Kannengiesser).

Much the same is true of today. If the Churches want to make a common confession, they must have the instrument which enables them to do so. They must develop new conciliar structures appropriate to the demands of our time. They must find ways of listening together to scripture and the tradition of the creeds, of living in real mutuality, mutual respect and mutual support—and ways of taking decisions together. The importance of such appropriate structures should not be underestimated. They may not guarantee the production of the creed, but their absence can certainly cripple the Church and prevent it from carrying out its task. Impressive theological achievements can remain ineffectual; even creeds of exemplary significance can go ignored because they lack authority.

So the question of new ecumenical creeds inevitably brings up the question of the magisterium. How can the Churches speak with one voice? How can an ecumenical magisterium come into being? Agreement would certainly be made easier if there were no longer an insistence on the Roman Catholic side on making the primacy and infallibility of the Pope an object of the Church's creed (Dulles). Then, however, procedures for common action would have to be found. Work on this problem is still in its initial stages. It is probably most likely to lead to results if it returns to the conciliar models of the early Church and draws inspiration from them.

### WHAT ARE THE IMMEDIATE STEPS?

What implications for the ecumenical movement follow from all these reflections? Two tasks come to mind, which must be undertaken in parallel.

## 1. The Reception of the Tradition

Every effort must be made to reach agreement about the sources on which the Church draws in confessing its faith today. What authority does scripture have in the life of the Church (Costas)? What significance do the creeds of the early Church possess?—and in this connection how should we assess the issue of the Filioque, which is still unresolved between East and West? What is the significance and place of baptism and the eucharist in the life of the Church? What part has the ministry to play? How are all these elements to be related to each other? A vast amount of theological work has already been done in the ecumenical movement on all these questions. The question is how the emerging consensus can become common tradition? Intellectual awareness of possible agreement does not in itself produce change. We must wait for the common tradition to begin to take shape in the various traditions. Working out a consensus on disputed questions, such as Scripture and tradition. the baptism of adults and the baptism of children and the presence of Christ in the eucharist, is the first step, but agreement will then have to find expression in liturgy, catechesis and the life of the Church. To mention only one example, it could be of far-reaching importance for agreement on the sources if all the Churches could agree to give the invocation of the Spirit, or epiclesis, its proper place in the celebration of baptism and the eucharist (Willis). Only through such steps will a common approach to the sources be made possible.

## 2. Anticipatory Common Confessions

It is clear that the common tradition can be recovered only gradually. The lived consensus must be extended step by step. The Churches, however, do not need to wait for the end of this process. Even now they can, and indeed must, take up the task of confessing the faith to their time. A common confession of the Gospel cannot wait until unity is achieved. The compelling occasion for a contemporary confession already exists in more and more situations.

Contemporary confession of the faith can take many forms. Worked out texts are not the only way. Witness can be given to the Gospel by signs, gestures or actions. Almost all the contributors to this volume stress that confessing the faith must today more than ever be part and parcel of the life and practice of the Church. Truth is made manifest, not just by orthodoxy, but just as much, and in some circumstances even more, by orthopraxis (Højen).

The more boldly the now separated Churches make up their minds to confess the faith together, the faster will community grow between them. The more reluctant and cautious they are, the more surely will they remain prisoners of inherited divisions.

This anticipatory confessing of the faith together also includes a willingness to examine and possibly to adopt the modern creeds of other Churches. Churches today can no longer ignore the creeds of other Churches simply because they are the creeds of other Churches.

They must take notice of them as directed at themselves. They must engage with them in the 'struggle for the right interpretation' as if they already lived in full communion with them. They can also have the freedom to adopt the creeds of other Churches and make them their own. They need not feel obliged to say what they have to say a second time in different words if it has already been adequately said by another Church. There is an example here too: important effects on the witness and unity of the Church in West Germany could follow from the Evangelical Church's action in considering how far it can adopt the declaration of the Roman Catholic Synod of Würzburg on hope (cf. Marlé).

## 3. On the Way to Conciliar Communion

Extension of agreement and confession of the faith in the actual situation: will these two lines ever meet? Will the communion which keeps on making a contemporary confession in the continuity of the tradition ever come into being? Who can know the answer? The goal at least is unequivocal. The two lines are intended to meet. The Churches are intended to come together in a way which enables them to bear common witness.

Much will depend on the seriousness with which the still separated Churches take the communion which already links them. There is an interaction between lived communion and confession of the faith. Communion is not just the fruit of common confession; it is the precondition for it. The Orthodox liturgy introduces the recitations of the creed with the words: 'Let us love, that we may confess the faith . . .' This formula expresses a profound truth. As long as communion has not been restored, the faith cannot really be confessed.

Let us love one another: for the separated Churches that means that they break down the walls and give greater and greater scope to fellowship, that they acquire the freedom to confess their sins and mistakes to each other and to forgive each other, that they make intercession for each other in the liturgy, that they give one another spiritual and material support in their weakness. Mutual love goes further. It is not through statements alone, but also through structures, that they will commit themselves not to separate from one another again. They will choose structures which favour the growth of fellowship, which even compel them to come closer to each other and, as far as possible, to anticipate that communion which is their goal. And their first question will be, not whether they may already enter into communion; instead they will let themselves be guided by the question whether they must continue to refuse it (Damaskinos). Mutual love allows no rest until eucharistic communion can be celebrated.

The goal of the ecumenical movement, visible unity in one faith and one eucharistic communion, can be described as conciliar communion. The Churches will reach this goal most quickly if they anticipate it now in resolutely lived pre-conciliar communion.

*Translated by Francis McDonagh*

# Contributors

KYUNG YUN CHUN is a Korean who was educated in Tokyo, and the USA. He is a Presbyterian minister and teaches at a seminary in South Korea. He has been a visiting professor in the USA and in Federal Germany. He was chairman of the committee for translation of the NT into Korean.

AVERY DULLES, S.J., has been professor of theology at the Catholic University of America since 1974. He is president-elect of the American Theological Society. He has published widely on apologetics and exegesis, revelation, dogma, models of the Church and the survival of the Church.

ORLANDO E. COSTAS is ordained a minister in the Baptist Church and the United Church of Christ. He teaches at the Seminario Biblio Latinoamericano in Costa Rica and Fuller Theological Seminary in Pasadena, California. He is the Protestant coordinator of the Project for the History of Theology and Philosophy in Latin America and has written extensively on third world theology themes.

ALASDAIR HERON is lecturer in Christian dogmatics at Edinburgh University. He is associate editor of the *Scottish Journal of Theology*. He has published widely on ecumenism, tolerance, toleration, and theology.

PEDER HØJEN teaches dogmatic theology and ecumenical theology at the Institute for Systematic Theology of Copenhagen University, Denmark, and is director of the Institute. He has published on, among other subjects, contemporary Catholicism and ecumenism.

CHARLES KANNENGIESSER, S.J., teaches patristics and the history of the origins of Christianity at the Institute Catholique in Paris. He is a member of the editorial committee of Recherches de Science Religieuse and literary director of Editions Beauchesne in Paris. He has published widely works in his field, among them studies of Athanasius, Chrysostom, Augustine and the belief in the resurrection.

BERNHARD LANG is professor of Old Testament studies and early Judaism at the Catholic theological faculty of the University of Tübingen, Federal Germany. He has published on exegesis, Wisdom, Ezekiel and other biblical topics.

HENK VAN DER LINDE was born in Utrecht, the Netherlands, and is professor for ecumenical studies at the Catholic University of Nijmegen.

RENE MARLE, S.J., is a professor at the Catholic Institute in Paris where he is in charge of the Higher Institute of Pastoral Catechetics. He has published widely on Bultmann and NT exegesis, hermeneutics, Bonhoeffer, Christian identity, and God-language.

RONALD MODRAS is a professor at St John's Seminary, Plymouth, Michigan, USA. He has published on unity, Tillich's theology of the Church, and human sexuality.

JÜRGEN MOLTMANN is a member of the Evangelical Reformed Church in Federal Germany. He is professor of systematic theology at Tübingen University. He has published several leading works on the theology of hope, predestination, anthropology, suffering and the Spirit.

DAMASKINOS PAPANDREOU is a Greek Orthodox priest. He was head of the secretariat for the preparation of the Orthodox Grand Council and a member of the Orthodox-Vatican council for the publication of official Roman-Constantinopolitan texts. He was appointed Metropolitan of Tranoupolis in 1970 and an extraordinary professor of Lucerne University, Switzerland in 1974.

OLIVER STRATFORD TOMKINS was Bishop of Bristol, UK, until 1975. He has been chairman of the Faith and Order Working Committee of the WCC and a member of the WCC Central Committee. He has published on the wholeness of the Church, unity, faith, and ecumenism.

LUKAS VISCHER is director of the Secretariat of the Commission on Faith and the Constitution of the WCC. He is a Swiss Protestant pastor. He has published on St Basil, confirmation, ecumenism, and is co-author of *The Common Catechism*.

DAVID WILLIS is professor of historical theology and church history at San Francisco Theological Seminary, and at the Graduate Theological Union, Berkeley, California, and the Charles Hodge professor of systematic theology at Princeton Theological Seminary. He was co-chairperson of official dialogues between the Vatican and the Reformed Churches.